"When you get labeled "the Discipleship Man" there is a reason for it. After reading *Christlike*, you will know why...on these pages, Bill Hull doesn't only share his latest, best thoughts and reflections, but takes us deep into his own journey...and it looks a lot like Jesus to me."

—DR. KEITH MEYER, pastor and author of *Whole Life Transformation: Becoming The Change Needed In Your Church* (InterVarsity Press, June of 2010)

"Bill Hull speaks directly from his heart and personal experience in his latest book, yet his words are based on a lifetime of ministry experience. *Christlike* is about a journey, Bill's own journey as he has come into a deeper and richer experience of discipleship to Jesus. Bill challenges all of us to lay aside simplistic formulaic approaches to the Christian life and instead, in a very uncomplicated way, allow Jesus to transform us from the inside out. This is an important book, from an important voice."

—MICHAEL J. WILKINS, PHD, distinguished professor of New Testament language and literature and dean of the faculty, Talbot School of Theology, Biola University; author of *Following the Master, In His Image*, and *Commentary on Matthew*

"Bill Hull understands that discipleship is not a program but a life-long journey of following Jesus. He opens our understanding of the gospel of the kingdom and then invites us to understand what it really means to be a disciple of Jesus. I love Bill's writing style, and I love the message of his book even more."

—ALAN ANDREWS, former U.S. director, The Navigators

Christlike

The Pursuit of Uncomplicated Obedience

BILL HULL

NAVPRESS

NavPress is the publishing ministry of The Navigators, an international Christian organization and leader in personal spiritual development. NavPress is committed to helping people grow spiritually and enjoy lives of meaning and hope through personal and group resources that are biblically rooted, culturally relevant, and highly practical.

For a free catalog go to www.NavPress.com
or call 1.800.366.7788 in the United States or 1.800.839.4769 in Canada.

© 2010 by Robert W. Hull

All rights reserved. No part of this publication may be reproduced in any form without written permission from NavPress, P.O. Box 35001, Colorado Springs, CO 80935. www.navpress.com

NAVPRESS and the NAVPRESS logo are registered trademarks of NavPress. Absence of ® in connection with marks of NavPress or other parties does not indicate an absence of registration of those marks.

ISBN: 978-1-60006-694-8

Cover design by Arvid Wallen
Cover imagery by Shutterstock

Some of the anecdotal illustrations in this book are true to life and are included with the permission of the persons involved. All other illustrations are composites of real situations, and any resemblance to people living or dead is coincidental.

Unless otherwise identified, all Scripture quotations in this publication are taken from the *Holy Bible*, New Living Translation (NLT), copyright © 2004. Used by permission of Tyndale House Publishers, Inc., Wheaton, Illinois 60189. All rights reserved. Other versions used include: the New American Standard Bible® (NASB), Copyright © 1960, 1962, 1963, 1968, 1971, 1972, 1973, 1975, 1977, 1995 by The Lockman Foundation. Used by permission; the *Holy Bible,* New International Version® (NIV®), Copyright © 1973, 1978, 1984 by International Bible Society, used by permission of Zondervan, all rights reserved; the Revised Standard Version Bible (RSV), copyright 1946, 1952, 1971, by the Division of Christian Education of the National Council of the Churches of Christ in the USA, used by permission, all rights reserved; and the King James Version (KJV).

Library of Congress Cataloging-in-Publication Data

Hull, Bill, 1946-
  Christlike : the pursuit of uncomplicated obedience / Bill Hull.
    p. cm.
  Includes bibliographical references (p.   ).
  ISBN 978-1-60006-694-8
  1. Christian life. 2. Obedience--Religious aspects--Christianity. I. Title.
  BV4647.O2H86 2010
  248.4--dc22
                                        2009037818

Printed in the United States of America

1 2 3 4 5 6 7 8 / 14 13 12 11 10

Other Books by Bill Hull

The Complete Book of Discipleship

Jesus Christ, Disciplemaker

The Disciple-Making Pastor

The Disciple-Making Church

Choose the Life: Exploring a Faith That Embraces Discipleship

Seven Steps to Transform Your Church

Building High Commitment in a Low-Commitment World

Revival That Reforms

Straight Talk On Spiritual Power

Anxious for Nothing

A Disciple's Guide to Choosing the Life

Experience the Life, Curriculum (with Paul Mascarella)

To Jane Marie Hull,

a true partner in the faith

Thanks to my editor, Liz Heaney, who made a significant contribution to this book. Her ability to get inside the writer's head and pull out the best is remarkable.

Contents

Introduction

A mind stretched by a new idea can never go back to its original dimensions.

— Oliver Wendell Holmes,
The Autocrat of the Breakfast Table

I want to change your mind. My goal is that after you have read this book, you won't be able to return your mind to its original shape. I am not trying to influence your thoughts on any small matter but on one that could revolutionize the course of your life. I want to change your mind about what it means to be a Christian.

I have been following Jesus for a very long time, yet I continue to learn new lessons that have required me to rethink my life. My struggle has been how to connect the private character issues of spirituality to the larger mission of what we have been told is our task: changing the world. Oliver Wendell Holmes reportedly said, "I don't give a fig for simplicity on this side of complexity, but I would give anything for simplicity on the other side of complexity." We live in a complex world, but I would like to help you emerge from this book with the simplicity of life and mission that is priceless.

Understanding the complexity of our world has become a challenge even to the greatest minds. Philosophers, historians, theologians, politicians, and even the media are stumped by the complex, web-like issues we face. Consider, for instance, the major issues facing the world: social injustice, political tyranny, hunger, poverty, and disease. Malaria, one of the most preventable diseases, is growing around the world because of the lack of clean water or effective pesticides that kill the mosquito larva. Much of the blame goes to evil governments led by tyrants who enrich themselves and starve their people. The infamous genocides in Rwanda and Darfur are not the end of such atrocities; many other less-publicized conflicts are continuing. As I write, the global financial community is locked in a crisis that threatens the sense of security we have known. People are both angry and afraid. Although the words written on the one dollar bill are, "In God we trust," our fear indicates that, in reality, money has been the object of our trust. This is even true of Christians.

One of life's great complexities is the question *Why was I born here and now?* For example, why am I not a blacksmith who was born in 1605 in the South, or a member of an Indian tribe in North America at the turn of the nineteenth century? When I look my dog in the eye, I wonder, *Why her instead of me?* You get the idea. Humanity has been asking these kinds of questions for centuries. While in Athens, the apostle Paul spoke on Mars Hill, a sort of town hall for intellectuals. He told his skeptical congregation this about these kinds of unanswerable conundrums:

From one man [God] created all the nations throughout the whole earth. He decided beforehand when they should rise and fall, and he determined their boundaries. His purpose was for the nations to seek after God and perhaps feel their way toward him and find him — though he is not far from any one of us. For in him we live and move and exist. . . . God overlooked people's ignorance about these things in earlier times, but now he commands everyone everywhere to repent of their sins and turn to him. For he has set a day for judging the world with justice by the man he has appointed, and he proved to everyone who this is by raising him from the dead. (Acts 17:26-28,30-31)

Simplicity is found in the understanding that God is the one who made the decision to create me here and now and determined that I would live in a certain place and be a certain height. (I won't blame him for the weight!) The conditions of our lives are from a divine decision. Why I wasn't born into a war-torn nation or why I didn't die of starvation at age four are questions far too complex for any human being to answer. However, what I am to do with the here and now of my life is simple. I am to be a Christ follower, and I will be held accountable for my actions. The complexity is that we don't know the details; the simplicity is that God made the choice and in him we live, move, and exist.

The simplicity on the other side of complexity is a person—a disciple—not a strategy or movement. Disciples are devoted to being "little Christs" in the world. Disciples have many different faces and skin colors, and they speak thousands of languages. Some scrape by for their daily bread, while others have way more than is necessary and don't know how to handle it. Some disciples are free to go to church; others must sneak there to pray and worship. Disciples live in Darfur; they have friends and family who have died of malaria or have been cut down in a tribal war. They work on Wall Street and were part of the recent financial meltdown. They are in the streets protesting the G8, the World Trade Organization, and the war in Iraq. They are walking through the marketplace in Bagdad with an American flag on their sleeves and rifles slung over their shoulders; they are working in the West Wing; they have an office in the United States Capitol with their name on the door. Some disciples are faithful, able to hold things together and resist the pressure to lie; others have sold out.

Will Christ's disciples save the world? No, not now, not under the current conditions. But we can save our worlds, the little space where we live and the people we touch. And if the millions who are disciples of a revolutionary named Jesus live the life Christ called them to live, then what Dallas Willard calls "the divine conspiracy"[1] will take effect. Like a healing tonic, it will wash over the world one person, one inch at a time. Love cannot be resisted.

C. S. Lewis lends a hand in clarifying what is needed: "The church exists for nothing else but to draw men into Christ, to make them little Christs. If they are not doing that, all the cathedrals, clergy, missions, sermons, even the Bible itself, are simply a waste of time. God became man for no other purpose."[2]

The goal of this book is to clarify the aim of the disciple's life. Discipleship has a simple aim, and you might be surprised to learn that it is not the church. The aim of discipleship is life; it is more about life on your street than what happens in church meetings. The actual result of being a disciple is that we influence others through our ordinary life. In John 10:10, Christ said, "I have come that they may have life, and have it to the full" (NIV). Can the ordinary life of a disciple be the key to affecting all of the surrounding culture? Yes, it can, and it must. The "abundant life," as older translations render it, is what will be described in this book as life in the kingdom. Life as God intended can be abundant only when Christ himself embodies us. When we follow Christ in discipleship, we grant permission for Christ to rule us. All that is included in Christ's rule—the fruit of the Spirit, the gifts of the Spirit, the guidance of the Spirit, the power of the Spirit—is present to influence the world around us. It is this quality in a person that makes transformation of culture possible.

When we lose discipleship, we lose the opportunity to teach people deeply. Spiritual formation, the end result of discipleship, is a deeper and more revolutionary change than mere conformity. It is much harder than getting people to externally conform. Revolution requires more than a series of external behaviors; the change must take hold on the inside. But this doesn't happen automatically. Real change is supernatural; it requires intentionality and is anything but passive. Nor is it quick and easy. If it were, then a commitment to discipleship and spiritual formation would be commonplace.

I believe that our consumerist, hyperactive, impatient church has hijacked the idea of spiritual formation. When we walk into the door of a local church, it seems as though we are in a negotiation mode: "God, how much of my life can I still control and yet reap all the benefits of submission?" Is there a way to address the inner life without being selfish? Is there a way to move Christians from being consumers predominately focused on self to being committed followers predominately focused on serving others? I think there is.

It is time to rethink what it means to be a Christian. It is time to rethink how, if we did become mature spiritual beings, we could affect the world.

Let's dive in.

CHAPTER 1

Rethinking What It Means to Be Christian

I was flying home after an intense four days of meeting with writers, pastors, and Christian leaders. I didn't want to talk; I wanted rest. My seatmate was already settled into 21A, with book in hand, earphones ready to listen to music after clearing ten thousand feet. I had my iPod and a book. So far so good. Then I made the mistake of saying hello. He nodded his head and looked away. Good. He wasn't one of those irritating chatterboxes.

But when the pilot came on to explain that our flight would be thirty minutes longer due to some thunderstorms in the area, my seatmate turned and asked, "So, what have you been doing in Minneapolis?" How do you explain that you have been meeting with some of the best thinkers in the land twice a year for five years in order to define the problem with the church? How could I condense all the nuance, debates, writing, praying, and discussions into a simple statement? After a moment's thought, I answered, "Well, we have been wondering if there is a problem with the church." He immediately laughed and said, "I grew up a Lutheran in Iowa. I know there is a problem!" Then he asked, "What did you find out?"

It had taken us ten meetings to define the problem, and he was asking me to condense our conclusions into a simple statement. I drew a breath and said, "The problem is that many of us have been taught and believe that we can become a Christian and not a disciple." His reply showed that he understood exactly what I meant: "You mean to say you believe but don't act like you believe? What is the solution?" This stranger had gone further in ten minutes than our group had in five years! "The solution," I answered, "is to rearrange our lives around the practices of Jesus so we will become authentic followers."

In years past, I would have whipped out my trusty *Four Spiritual Laws* tract and proceeded to win my seatmate for Christ. But God had been doing so much in me that I wanted to just step into the doorway my seatmate offered, so I said something that I would not have said before: "I have spent a lot of my life trying to make things happen and trying to get the people around me to do what they didn't want to do or didn't have the character to do. I've decided to stop trying to change the world on my own. I've even stopped trying to force change on the church. I have decided to focus on changing me. I've hit a lot of walls in my life and have hurt a lot of people. I'm finished with that. I just want people to be attracted to Christ because of who I am, what I have to say, and the way I say it."

My seatmate turned away from me and looked out the window. I saw his face tighten and his skin redden. He swallowed hard as his shoulders slumped, and he began to cry. Then he began to weep. I didn't know what to do, so I quietly waited. He began to tell me about the many walls he had hit, and as we talked, he found new hope in the gospel—a gospel that came to him with humility and in authenticity. I don't believe that this man had heard the spirit of the gospel until that moment, and it was only because of my ongoing personal transformation. Transformation is the vehicle through which we need to deliver the gospel. If the message is fresh and current, then it will punch through the wall between people and knock down the barriers and defenses that the Enemy constructs to keep it from those who need it.

But as my seatmate understood, the problem in the church is that far too many Christians don't act like they believe. It is time to rethink the gospel itself and the ways we become spiritual.

One Gospel, Many Approaches

The term *gospel* is so common that it creates different meanings to different hearers. It has been said that the gospel is so simple a child can understand it but so deeply profound the greatest minds have yet to plumb its depth. So let's take a look at what is meant by the gospel.

The Greek word itself is *euaggelion*, which means good news. The New Testament authors used it ninety-five times and assumed that their readers would know what they meant by it. The apostle Paul claimed that God himself had revealed the meaning to him,[1] and he warned that anyone who would pervert it and teach it differently would go to hell. His statement as to the identity of the gospel is found in his letter to the Corinthians:

> I delivered to you as of first importance what I also received, that Christ died for our sins in accordance with the scriptures, that he was buried, that he was raised on the third day in accordance with the scriptures, and that he appeared to Cephas, then to the twelve. Then he appeared to more than five hundred brethren at one time, most of whom are still alive, though some have fallen asleep. (1 Corinthians 15:3-6, RSV)

Some have claimed there are different gospels, one for the individual and another for communities or nations. Others have said that Jesus taught one version and Paul another. But Paul claimed there was only one gospel and that his gospel was the same as what Jesus and the apostles in Jerusalem taught. He wrote, "Whether then it was I or they, so we preach and so you believed" (1 Corinthians 15:11, RSV).

There is just one gospel, but as the late missionary statesman and scholar Lesslie Newbigin astutely observed, "No gospel is pure; it is always embodied in a culture."[2] So we tailor the gospel to various cultures and for different audiences. Paul even mentioned there was the gospel of the circumcised and that of the uncircumcised. He was entrusted with taking the message to the Gentiles, while Peter primarily was preaching to the Jews. This analysis might have been a snapshot rather than trend, because we know that later in his life, Peter ministered broadly (see Galatians 1:8; 2:7).

We also focus on a certain part of the gospel message and its many applications, depending on who is on the receiving end. When Paul tailored his message to the philosophers in Athens, he was attempting to find some common ground on which to start the Athenians thinking with him. At that time, Greek philosophy was in decline. Aristotle and Plato had crafted a theology of the First Mover god, who was detached; the second-level god, Demiurge, was the active god. This may be why Paul used poetry and philosophical argument in his appeal to them. His approach on Mars Hill differed from his hearings before the Roman judges Felix, Festus, and Agrippa as well as the people in Jerusalem.[3] In those cases, Paul gave his personal story and made no philosophic statements nor employed any poetry. So it could be proposed that there is only one gospel but many ways to talk about it, depending on your hearer. Nowadays we call this packaging. Pastor Tim Keller says he preaches both the circumcised and the uncircumcised, or the believer and unbeliever, gospel in New York City and allows each group to overhear what he says to the other group.[4]

The Importance of Getting It Right

But what is the gospel? How we answer is crucial because it determines what kind of people we become. What we are becoming governs what we are doing. This includes the reputation we have, the mission we undertake, and whether the community of faith is a self-indulgent crowd or a sacrificial force for good. Many today tend to separate the idea of salvation from behavior and reputation. "Christians are not perfect, just forgiven," says the bumper sticker. This sentiment seems to be more of an excuse than an explanation of grace. Salvation is seen as a way to get into heaven.

I cannot overstate the importance of getting the gospel right and then applying it correctly. This is at the root of the American problem that has caused the church to fade in its impact. The church's drive to be relevant has diminished the distinction between the church and the culture. And when that difference gets too narrow, the church disappears into the gloaming that John called "the world."

There are at least five gospels with significant following that are being preached in the United States. Each is creating a certain kind of person and church. In this chapter and the next, we'll take a look at these and the kind of Christian each creates.

The Forgiveness-Only Gospel

Years ago, a well-meaning parishioner invited me to lunch. He wanted to take me aside to clue me in on doing a better job. About the time I had the spaghetti wrapped around my fork and on its way to my mouth, he spat out, "You're not preaching the gospel!" I was not sure what he meant, as I was preaching through Romans verse by verse, so I swallowed the pasta and followed it up with a meatball before I challenged his assessment. "Hey, I am teaching the gospel in great detail, so what do you mean?" "That's not the gospel. People aren't getting saved; no one is coming forward for salvation. You're not telling them what they need to hear in order to trust Christ." He sat back, satisfied that he had gotten it all out.

Bingo! Now I knew what he meant. He was into the CliffsNotes version of the gospel, the one that gives you four quick facts and into heaven you go. Say a quick prayer at the end of church, and you will get your pass into heaven and not even be late for lunch. I explained that we had a ministry time at the end of the service with trained prayer counselors and that many people had prayed to commit their lives to Christ. It is just that we didn't announce it; we didn't put a gold sticker on their chests and put them in a display window. But for many Christians, the "get them into the fold as quickly and efficiently as possible" model has come to mean the gospel. They think this method and condensed model is what Paul and others lived and died for.

Unfortunately, this formula has made it so easy to get into the Christian life that it has made it almost impossible for people to *live* the Christian life. The reason? This gospel is only about agreement with a set of religious facts. It acts as an electronic bar code that beeps when it recognizes the right image. This gospel encourages people to recite words they don't understand and have no plan to do anything about. It's the gospel of Michael Corleone in the child baptism scene in the film *The Godfather* when he renounces the Devil while his henchman kills the heads of the rival Mafia families. This gospel is a two-story philosophical house. The lower story is the rational world, the upper story the metaphysical one, and they don't have to match. Proponents of this gospel are looking for a way to cover all their bases, to please their family, and to get a religious edge on life. It is a very large category indeed.

The root problem of the forgiveness-only gospel is that it tends to create Christians who don't feel the need to follow Christ. This gospel tends to teach that entrance into salvation is the finish line; the great moment is over. Game, set, match. All future effort or work for Christ and his church is optional. It is great if you can do it, but it's not really needed. After all, there is always a minority of Christians who get the discipleship gene, the sacrificial gene, the service gene, and they carry the load. This gospel is a natural breeding ground for casual Christianity.

I am not saying that pastors teach this gospel on purpose; I believe that it is taught by default. But the way the Christian life is explained makes a huge difference in expectation and effort. Is it described as an event or a journey? Is grace just for guilt, or is it something needed daily? Is the gospel about my status alone or about how I interact with others? Because of the efforts of mass evangelism, televangelism, and the need for immediate results, "getting saved" dominates the salvation landscape. The call to discipleship and the need to be spiritually formed are overwhelmed with getting people in the door. Ironically, this and the emphasis on being relevant have resulted in a church in decline, both numerically and morally.

This gospel limits grace to the forgiveness of sin; it teaches that faith is agreement with a set of facts, and it allows discipleship to be optional. It most naturally creates a church largely populated by casual Christians with a minority of serious ones who somehow survive the initiation. Although there are many solid and faithful members of Christian communities who are products of such a gospel, there is also an underlying resistance to absolute surrender that is part human nature, part theology. The lingering effect of this theology is that effort—work, discipline, duty, and self-sacrifice—are somehow anti-thetical to grace. Since the opposite is true, this gospel rips the heart out of the Christian faith; it makes cheap what cost God everything. As Dietrich Bonhoeffer declared with such gentility, "We must drive a stake through its heart."[5]

The Gospel of the Left

This is not about the political left per se; it is about the liberal world-view that includes philosophy, the arts, theology, and politics. It falls into two categories: the old religious left and the neo-religious left.

The Old Religious Left

When I think of the old religious left, my memory takes me back to 1973, when I was twenty-seven and without a seminary degree. The search committee for an American Baptist church of two hundred adults was interviewing me in consideration as their pastor. My hunch was they wanted to practice their interviewing skills on me. When they asked me about women in ministry, I presented the straightforward teaching of Paul that women should not hold authority over men and that wives were helpmates and should submit to their husband's author-ity.[6] The reaction was immediate. One young man scoffed and several protested out of turn. The chairman had to quiet members down. I was thinking, *Aren't these people Baptist? I thought Baptists believed the Bible!* Obviously, these Baptists didn't. The members of this search committee believed in some of it, the part that didn't violate their social sensibilities. They were characteristic of many liberals during that most turbulent part of the women's movement, when to be a politically left Christian meant you had to find creative ways to adjust your view of Scripture in order to accommodate your personal awakening.

The roots of old liberalism are to be found in nineteenth-century Europe and the advent of what was called "higher criticism." It questioned the veracity of the New Testament text and taught that the Bible had been redacted and different authors wrote it than were claimed by the Bible itself. These liberals also questioned the Virgin Birth and miracles of Jesus; they claimed that Paul didn't like women and that the prophecies Jesus fulfilled were added after he fulfilled them in order to make them look divine in origin. Most of the proponents of such deconstructive ideas were not evil; they were people of Christian faith who had good intentions.

Theologian Rudolf Bultmann and his fellow German brigade of Karl Barth, Emil Brunner, and Dietrich Bonhoeffer have been demonized in many a conservative classroom. They were not that liberal. Barth in particular moved the entire European Church from left to the middle into what has been called Neo-Orthodoxy. These were devout men who were trying to make the gospel more relevant to their culture. Bonhoeffer was not an evangelical, but he was a passionate disciple of Jesus whose writings have helped millions. Bultmann is best known for his essay to pastors delivered in lecture form in Frankfurt in 1941. In the lecture, he presented his idea for removing the impossible in order to believe myths recorded in Scripture. His passion was to encourage the proclamation of the gospel in terms that modern society could accept. To this end, he introduced a new method of biblical interpretation to the theological world that would divest the New Testament of its primitive worldview. He didn't suggest removing the miracles; he recommended finding ways of talking about God's mystery in human terms.

Walter Rauschenbusch, the father of the social gospel, was a theological liberal but was motivated as a Baptist pastor to make the gospel work in New York's Hell's Kitchen. His book *Christianity and the Social Crisis* sold over fifty thousand copies in 1907. Like many movements, the social gospel makes sense in the context of serious Christians attempting to meet people's needs and understand their own message. Rauschenbusch drew some of his thinking from two famous liberal German professors at the University of Berlin, Albrecht Ritschl and Adolf Harnack. I can't resist the aside that Bonhoeffer, as a young student, rode the train to the University of Berlin with Adolf Harnack, a family friend. The old professor befriended, protected, and taught the boy who would become a great teacher and leader. Because of the German influence, the social gospel became the prominent philosophy among more liberal church and political leaders. Rauschenbusch's not-so-liberal views were assimilated into a much more liberal church. He died in 1918, but his philosophy morphed into the new bastions of liberalism.

In the 1930s, ground zero for old liberalism in the United States was Union Theological Seminary in New York City, along with the divinity schools of the Ivy League. The ministry of the old theological left was to take the teachings of Jesus to the street, to make the message of social justice relevant to the common person. Renowned theologian Reinhold Niebuhr was a major part of such an effort. Niebuhr was a theological rock star in the 1950s; he appeared on the cover of *Time* magazine and was a regular interviewee on nationally broadcast news programs. He was loved by the left for his sophistication and subtle ways of putting down Billy Graham and other conservative Christians.

The "social gospel" was the term people gave to the idea that you help people in need but you don't burden them with accountability to the gospel message, including the need to repent of sin and follow Christ. The part that the old religious left got right was the need to organize compassion by helping people in need. What they got wrong was the abandonment of the spiritual side of the gospel as it relates to the soul. I might add that what they have lacked is the passion and confidence to believe in the uniqueness of Jesus and his message. The left deconstructed the Bible, leaving it as an unreliable book of mythical stories that never occurred. Its relevance was in the underlying or spiritual meaning of such myths as the Resurrection and the Second Coming. The Resurrection is a new attitude and the Second Coming an inspirational political leader. This morphed into liberation theology, which was Marxism dressed in religious vestments.

Many mainline churches in America that hold to such views are dying and are in large part on life support. The urge to be relevant and inclusive is not sufficient reason to defrock Scripture of its authority. When that happens, people don't have a place to stand, a safe place to moor in a storm, or a reason to hope. The teaching of the religious left has created people who attempt to behave like Christians without becoming Christians.

I find it interesting that in the twenty-first century, Rauschenbusch's philosophy is being practiced more by evangelicals than anyone else. The liberal church is in serious decline, whereas the evangelical church still has vigor.

The Neo-Religious Left

The neo-religious left is more evangelical and has not been as aggressive in the deconstruction of the Bible. They have been more inclined to call for a new hermeneutic, a new way to interpret the Scriptures. That is code for trying to figure out some new interpretations because they don't like the ones we now have. A well-known author, speaker, and pastor has called for a more large-hearted orthodoxy because, as he alleges, the ancient one no longer speaks to the problems we face. In the last few years, he has moved more to the left theologically. My purpose is not to pick this man apart. I believe he is a good thinker and asks important questions. I am concerned, however, with the gospel he is proposing.

In his most recent book, he confronts the reader with the big questions:

> What are the biggest problems in the world? . . . I mean problems that cause the most suffering in the present, that pose the greatest threat to our future, that cause most of the other problems, that lie at the root of what's wrong with the world?

He points out that we have four crises: a prosperity crisis, equity crisis, security crisis, and spirituality crisis. The crises in prosperity, equity, and security are economic in that our global economy cannot sustain life within desired environmental limits. There is a growing gap between the rich and poor, and this creates fear and anger. Because people are at the opposite ends of the economic spectrum, this can lead to conflict and war. The fourth crisis of the spirit is a failure of our "framing story," particularly Christianity's, to offer a solution that is as big as the problem.

The author goes on to advocate that we go beyond the limits of our present story to find a "fresh vision of our religion's founder and his message." The theme that runs through this kind of thinking says, "The Christians who have lived the previous two thousand years didn't have to face the complexities we face today. So we need to find a new 'framing story,' or a more inclusive, generous orthodoxy, to address the global crisis we face. We need a gospel that provides hope and answers to the issues we face. We need to go beyond the premodern orthodoxy, because in order to be relevant, we need new answers."

Let the deconstruction begin. This author also talks about the Fall as "consumption beyond limits." He says that hell, literal or figurative, is for the "rich and comfortable who proceed on their way without concern for their poor neighbor day after day" and challenges the conventional idea that the gospel is about the sin problem. He says that when we focus on the sin problem, we relegate Jesus to a practical irrelevance in relation to human social problems and hope of the afterlife tends to be an opiate that numbs us to the social ills that surround us. He goes on to call the atonement "divine child abuse" and says that the idea of hell is God's solving the problem of evil with violence. He says,

> This eschatological understanding of a violent second coming leads us to believe [as we've said before] that in the end, even God finds it impossible to fix the world apart from violence and coercion; no one should be surprised when those shaped by this theology behave accordingly. If we remain charmed by this kind of eschatology, we will be forced to see the nonviolence of the Jesus of the Gospels as a kind of strategic fake-out, like a feigned retreat in war, to be followed up by a crushing blow of so-called redemptive violence in the end. The gentle Jesus of the first coming becomes a kind of trick Jesus, a fake-me-out Messiah, to be replaced by the true jihadist Jesus of a violent second coming. [7]

Yes, this interpretation will require a new hermeneutic indeed, possibly a new Bible, one rewritten for the post-rational mind.

The new left claims to believe the Bible but says it needs to be interpreted in a new way. The new left is deconstructing the old hermeneutic for the sake of relevance. While well intentioned, they are making the same mistake the old left made. The ultimate problem is that after you have deconstructed and reconstructed with a new, inclusive Jesus—a Jesus who doesn't go to war, who doesn't believe in hell, a Jesus of no consequences and who whimsically hopes evil will go quietly into the night—who wants to follow such a flaccid leader, let alone God? We don't need a God who negotiates with evil. This kind of thinking creates well-meaning Christians who, like parents who negotiate with a rebellious child rather than introduce the child to reality, believe that kindness and appeasement can erase evil. Rather, we need a God who will crush evil and eliminate it from creation (see Romans 1:18-32).

Phyllis Tickle, one of the most respected speakers and writers on religion in America, has written a book that provides a theory of where the new left is going. In her engaging work *The Great Emergence*, she attempts to craft a new vision for the church's future. Her thesis is that every five hundred years, the church cleans out its attic and throws out what is not working or isn't needed anymore—a giant rummage sale if you will. The first era was the formation of Christianity, its doctrines, its organization and culture. This era ended around the sixth century with the rise of Gregory the Great. As Pope, he empowered the monastic movement, which held Christianity in trust for five hundred years. This was primarily because the barbarians who replaced the Romans were illiterate. In order to live, Christianity requires literacy because it is a religion of the book. The monastics were part of the 5 percent of the population who could read and write. They are legendary for their dedicated custodianship of the biblical manuscripts. The third era (called the Great Schism)—when the church divided east and west, Rome and Constantinople—was around 1054. It was the era of the crusades and almost a thousand years before the church reconciled. The next era, around 1517, was the Great Reformation. This protest movement ignited by Martin Luther's nailing of his ninety-five theses on the church door in Wittenberg, Germany, created the Protestant church.

It is not controversial to agree with Tickle that each of these eras were important turning points in church history. In each of these eras, the church threw out ideas or doctrines that no longer served to be helpful. But I do question her conviction that the next great era is the Great Emergence. She contends that in every case when the church threw off antiquated teachings, they were free to leap ahead and expand. The issue now is what is in the attic that needs to be thrown out?

Tickle skillfully tells the story of what needs to go and, according to her, is being cleaned out of the Christian attic. Columbus failed to fall off the edge of the flat earth, and then Copernicus proved the earth was round and that it rotated around the sun. Darwin provided an alternative story of origins, Freud and Jung a different explanation for human behavior. Tickle gives great importance to Joseph Campbell, for many years an influential scholar in the field of comparative mythology and comparative religion. Campbell is best known for the PBS series with Bill Moyers titled *The Power of Myth*. You may hear many people advocating that we "follow our bliss." This is the practical application of Campbell's thinking. Campbell's book *The Hero with a Thousand Faces* puts Christianity in its place as one of the world's great stories but essentially a myth. The series still stands as the most popular PBS has produced. Tickle concludes,

> The popularity of *The Power of Myth* rested certainly on its excellence and in part on Moyer's genius as well as Campbell's. . . . It triggered a whole new generation of expanded readership for Campbell's books; and together, books and series persuaded much of North American Christendom that exclusivity and particularity were a hard if not impossible sell. What of *solus christus*, not to mention *sola scriptura*.[8]

The two doctrines that distinguish Christianity and what it stands upon—that Christ is the unique way to God and the Scriptures are the revealed will of God—are now being discarded. Tickle believes that the Protestant teaching on homosexuality will also be thrown out "and that scripture will hold some authority but that the nature of that authority will be either dead or in mortal need of reconfiguration."[9] She adds that the idea that atonement is a requirement of an angry God who demands appeasement is also something that is going to be reconsidered. Then there is hell, which the new left considers to be something of an eternal overkill for a seventy-year blip on the divine calendar. If Tickle's assessment is correct, out in the trash will go: (1) the exclusivity of Christ, (2) the absolute authority of the Bible, (3) the substitutionary atonement for human sin, (4) hell as a place or eternal condition for the unbeliever, and (5) the interpretations of Scripture passages that define homosexuality and abortion as wrong. Tickle's summary is chilling:

> If . . . the Great Emergence really does what most of its observers think it will, it will rewrite Christian theology—and thereby North American culture—into something far more Jewish, more paradoxical, more narrative, and more mystical than anything the Church has had for the last seventeen or eighteen hundred years.[10]

The gospel of the new left is one of accommodation and capitulation to the surrounding culture. It should be remembered that its motivation is to seek God in a more personal way and to be relevant to the watching world. With that I can agree, but its abandonment of logic, its belief that truth is a social construct, and its epistemology that truth cannot be known on the human level make it a house built on sinking sand.

This gospel creates people who believe there is a greater truth above and beyond normal truth and that anyone who believes in knowable truth is arrogant and a product of modernity. Humility then is not knowing; if you can't know, then you don't need to decide about right or wrong; therefore, you are excused from commitment. Or the commitment is not to judge and not to be committed to any one truth that you would die for or live for. This gospel suspends the conventional laws of logic and rejects the law of noncontradiction. The law of logic states simply that if A is true, then B is untrue. So all religions can be wrong, but only one can be right, since they teach contradictory things. The neo-religious left has deconstructed language and made it merely semantics and symbols. Truth to them is socially constructed and, therefore, relative. The orthodox version of the gospel and interpretation of Scripture is culturally bound and, therefore, relative. It is what people thought before Galileo, Darwin, Freud, Marx,

Nietzsche, and company. Historically it has been held that truth is universal and absolute. It is unchanging; it is knowable. The neo-religious left believe that you can be two different things at once.

I believe that this gospel naturally creates people who are so inclusive that they have no stomach for truth. They do have a strong sense of the obvious: They have a strong sense of human rights (unless the subject is abortion), a strong sense of justice (unless it requires the death penalty), a powerful instinct to protect children (unless it calls for censorship of the Internet), and finally, an abounding faith in truth (as long as it is science). They are so tolerant that they have no standards that apply to everyone and are so confused about what is true that they have little confidence in their way of life and lack certitude about their eternal home. As an absolutist regarding truth, I say that the world, even in all its mystery, doesn't hang together without a reliable God, a trustworthy Scripture, and a hope grounded in the knowable Christ revealed in the Bible. Finally, this gospel gives us the liberal church, which is going, going, gone, much like a foul ball leaves the field of play. Liberal church attendance is now at its lowest level in fifty years.[11] Sadly, in the name of relevance, the evangelical left is moving closer to the liberal way of thinking and belief system.

The Prosperity Gospel

The Charismatic Movement is larger than its stepchild, the prosperity gospel. However, it would be fair to say that the prosperity teaching represents a significant percentage of the larger movement. Its leaders and writers fully support the deity of Christ and the authority of Scripture. Its distinctive is the belief that prosperity is both spiritual and physical. To be more precise, it teaches that the physical blessings of health and wealth are as sure as the saving of the soul. To go a bit deeper, this theology holds that atonement (what God has provided in the Cross) includes physical and financial blessing. It bases this belief on three converging Scriptures: Isaiah 53:4-6, 1 Peter 2:24, and Matthew 8:16-17.

It was our weaknesses he carried;
    it was our sorrows that weighed him down.
And we thought his troubles were a punishment from God,
    a punishment for his own sins!
But he was pierced for our rebellion,
    crushed for our sins.
He was beaten so we could be whole.
    He was whipped so we could be healed.
All of us, like sheep, have strayed away.
    We have left God's paths to follow our own.
Yet the Lord laid on him
    the sins of us all. (Isaiah 53:4-6, emphasis added)

He personally carried our sins
    in his body on the cross
so that we can be dead to sin
    and live for what is right.
By his wounds
    you are healed. (1 Peter 2:24)

That evening many demon-possessed people were brought to Jesus. He cast out the evil spirits with a simple command, and he healed all the sick. This fulfilled the word of the Lord through the prophet Isaiah, who said,

"He took our sicknesses
    and removed our diseases." (Matthew 8:16-17)

I agree with the idea that physical healing is included in the finished work of Christ. Where else could it come from? It is part of what God has provided. But I also believe that the healing of diseases of both mind and body may not happen on our timetable, or even in this life. It is a huge leap from a promise in the future to a guarantee here and now. While the idea that God will heal us in answer to prayer is not controversial, the idea that he has guaranteed it if we pray in faith is. Yes, there are some obvious barriers to answered prayer, such as unconfessed sin, lack of submission, and so on, but other reasons as to why God does not heal us now are a mystery. Many who have been faithful in their walk with God have not been healed from illness, such as the apostle Paul. The classic teaching has been that you need to confess your sin, strengthen your faith, give your money, and cast out the relevant demon and the door to healing will open.

The Charismatic Movement is the fastest growing part of the church worldwide. I became a Christian at a Charismatic university and believe this movement is a true gift to the church in that we have learned from it a great deal about worship and the work of the Spirit. It's also true that many people are now healed physically because they have come in contact with the people of this belief. My critique is focused on those in the movement who make the prosperity doctrine a centerpiece of their teaching. Now for the kind of disciple the prosperity gospel naturally produces.

Disciples Vulnerable to Exploitation

The majority of television preachers, especially those who have fallen from grace, have been prosperity focused. This should be no surprise, as money and power are corrupting elements. As that gloomy British historian Thomas Carlyle said years ago, "For every man who can stand prosperity, there are nine who cannot." The theology of the prosperity gospel espouses that material blessing is one of the ways you know that God is blessing you. That is why too many proponents of this gospel live in the palatial homes, own a fleet of cars, wear Armani suits, and adorn themselves with jewelry. Wealth is their bona fêtes, the evidence that their walk matches their talk. They live the myth before the public, and then they invite others to join in by sending in their "seed" so it will grow into something much larger.

What makes the prosperity message so insidious is that there are blessings in doing what it advocates. God does bless those who give, so there are cases when people get a financial blessing as a result. There is also the straight-up spiritual blessing, the sense of well-being that comes from giving. This theology is an exercise in sophistry; it appears to be true but isn't. The exploitation is that people do it under false pretenses, believing that there is a direct cause and effect, that "you get what you give." They think they will be healed or that their debt will be removed because they gave to the presenter's ministry. They climb out on the limb of faith recommended by the preacher, give their gift, believe with all their hearts, and then the limb breaks. They are not healed, so they land with a thud. This leads to disciples who carry the banner of the prosperity doctrine but live under a more practical gospel that reflects their reality. They have an uneasiness in their "spiritual gut" that what they report to be true actually isn't.

Disciples Who Feel Entitled

This gospel also creates people who "name it, claim it." The reasoning goes, "God has promised to provide all these benefits for us. We need to name our need and claim the benefit." Some will even contend that God has no choice in the matter. If he promises something in his Word, then we can speak it into existence. We can command it; it is ours.

The hubris is startling. There is a sense in which the belief that "God owes us something" is just a way of managing God and our own lives. I don't believe there is much submission or humility in this. It is the strong arm of the flesh attempting to get the results we crave.

Disciples Who Separate Spiritual Power and Spiritual Maturity

I taught in Charismatic colleges and seminaries and wrote a book that expresses my viewpoints on the range of issues regarding spiritual power.[12] The prosperity wing of the movement has an interesting distinction: It does not see a direct link between being filled with the Spirit and spiritual maturity. The belief is that the "baptism of the Spirit," which is usually accompanied by speaking in tongues, is primarily about spiritual power for ministry. The unleashing of gifts is for evangelism and for reaching people with the gospel. This is based on the passages in the New Testament that talk about signs and wonders and the role they played in advancing the church (see Acts 2:43; 5:12; 6:8; 7:36; Hebrews 2:4).

I think that being filled with the Holy Spirit does provide the power for ministry, but I find the prosperity movement's lack of connection to character and spiritual formation to be dangerous. When you have power without humility, it's like you are walking around with nitroglycerin in your pocket. It causes an explosion. Of course, there are humble leaders and members in the prosperity wing of the body. God seems to be able to break through barriers to form his people. But this is in spite of this gospel's natural tendency to create followers who focus on the power, the gifts, and the goodies, without the slow but urgent journey of being shaped into the image of Christ. Jesus lived and taught a gospel of humility, submission, obedience, and sacrifice (see Philippians 2:3-13).

The Consumer Gospel

The consumer gospel is by far the most pervasive and popular of the five gospels being preached in the United States today. This gospel combines the appeal for forgiveness with the abdication of any obligation of discipleship. It emphasizes the confession of sins for salvation. Everything else is off the table—following Christ, a lifelong commitment to discipleship—they are all optional. The idea that the Christian life is one of being a "living sacrifice" is secondary to salvation. This gospel rushes naturally into the waiting arms of self-interest.

We live in a world of consumption, assertiveness, speed, and fame. Impatience is the most accepted sin in Western culture. We are an impetuous people. This impatience not only is accepted in the church but is considered a positive quality among church leaders. According to the consumer gospel, everything must be faster and bigger. Impatience is presented as a sign of holy dissatisfaction, which drives the leaders to take church to the next level. Every year must bring net growth with new and exciting programs to keep consumer Christians with short attention spans interested.

The problem with impatience is that it short-circuits the forming of Christ in persons. The consumer mentality does not foster a life of submission and humility. It is a world where activity, including church, orbits around the individual. The mania for success trains people to think in terms of programs and gives them a short-term view of personal development. They begin to think, *If I can get a handle on this character flaw of uncontrolled anger in the next two months, then it will be taken care of. If it doesn't work, then I need to find a better teacher, church, curriculum, husband, wife, workplace.* In other words, *Change my circumstances, change me.*

This is a gospel of speed and fame; it is a natural by-product of our culture, which is driven by the mania to succeed. The consumer gospel produces disciples who behave like consumers. Their vocabulary is laden with phrases like, "We are looking for a church where we can be fed." Many appear to think of themselves as helpless little birds waiting in the nest with mouths open in anticipation of Mother dropping in a worm. They are preoccupied with the youth program, type of music, times and length of services, and personalities of the clergy. These folks leave churches because they are bored, or don't cry enough, or laugh enough, or tingle when the music plays. But what are we to do with a generation of church attendees who have been trained to measure their spirituality by what they thought of the worship service? Their language rarely reveals any interest in being challenged and accountable for spiritual life and service. When was the last time you heard someone complaining, "We left our church because when I volunteered to feed the hungry or nurse the sick I was turned away"?

This gospel is a product of the Enlightenment and its subsequent individualism. It is a reflection of our culture and is driven by the consumerism in which we have been trained. We are taught from birth to think about how everything around us can serve us and meet our needs. We have been trained to listen through marketing filters. Everything is for sale. These churches promise members, "If you use our products, you will be happy, healthy, and powerful." This is sort of like saying that if you wear a certain brand of shoes, you will be able to play in the NBA. The Christian message is the antithesis of that, but I am afraid it has largely succumbed to the enchanting message of the consumer gospel.

I agree with Tyler Wigg-Stevenson, who writes, "This should concern us because of the problems it creates for discipleship. Consumerism isn't just a social phenomenon — it's spirituality. And it comes with spiritual habits and disciplines that conflict with the particular practices of the Christian life."[13] Those habits are to treat Christian practices as optional and as the discipline of never fully committing to anything. The consumer gospel does not welcome discipleship, the intentional commitment to follow Jesus and live for others. That is why Dallas Willard has said,

> Why Christian faith has failed to transform the masses and to make a more just and peaceful world is because it has failed to transform the human character. The reason is that our gospel most often has not been accompanied by discipleship. Discipleship is not an essential part of Christianity today, in philosophy, program or curriculum.[14]

In other words, the majority of Christian leaders do not have a clear biblical explanation of what a disciple is and how it fits their mission ("in philosophy"). Consequently, their churches don't offer activities that lead others into discipleship ("in program"), nor does their teaching content and associated tools ("in curriculum").

Reflections

Most American Christians adopt one of the four gospels mentioned in this chapter. Usually, it means some hybrid of the four. The most common hybrid is a melding of the forgiveness-only gospel and the consumer gospel. This most often creates disciples who live by formulas and who interpret the Christian message as primarily a narrative about their own needs. The world is in orbit around the individual's need for personal peace and affluence.

However, if the early church had believed and preached such a gospel, it would never have gotten off the ground. If we do not preach the gospel that embraces the full range of God's work on earth, we cannot naturally progress into the kind of people God designed us to be. More important, if we don't live in the reality of that gospel, we will not be able to persuade others to join us. We will find ourselves trapped in little enclaves of the evangelical subculture that believe that the only thing that counts is "saving souls" and "church work." Additionally, we will not be able to complete our personal or corporate mission to the world.

Sociologist Rodney Stark begins his book *The Rise of Christianity* by addressing this crucial issue: "All questions concerning the rise of Christianity are one: How was it done? How did a tiny and obscure messianic movement from the edge of the Roman Empire dislodge classical paganism and become the dominant faith of Western civilization."[15] This is exactly the question to ask of the church at this point in history. At the beginning of Christianity, something took hold of believers on the inside, and it created a revolution. The life of God invaded humans and took up residence inside them.

We need to think more broadly, to wonder how the presence of God among his people would manifest itself if Christians allowed Christ to rule in every area of life. What would Christ's presence look like in the halls of Congress, the public classroom, or the university lecture hall? Is there any application of the gospel to the people of the earth that is not attached to the requirement to trust in Christ? Does God intend for his people and their message to do good for others even though they never become Christian? If the answer is yes, what might that gospel be? The next chapter explores these questions.

CHAPTER 2

The Gospel of the Kingdom

When the thief on the cross asked Jesus for help, he said, "Remember me when you come into your Kingdom" (Luke 23:42). This tells me that an unsophisticated criminal, an unlettered man, understood kingdom. He could have just read the sign posted on the top of Jesus' cross, "King of the Jews," but in Jesus' day the kingdom was a straightforward concept. It is interesting how complex we have made it. I recall reading volumes on the subject in seminary, and everyone had an opinion.

The concept of the kingdom is rooted in the ancient world of the Old Testament. Israel was a kingdom and was ruled by Saul, David, and Solomon in all their glory. When Jesus came into the kingdom of Israel, it no longer had a king. The country was dominated by the secular giant that was Rome and the Greco-Roman world. Jesus as Messiah, the Anointed One, came to fulfill the promise given to David that a new King would come and that Israel would once again have a King of kings who would rule from Jerusalem. So when Jesus spoke about his mission, he said things like, "I must preach the Good News of the Kingdom of God in other towns, too, because that is why I was sent" (Luke 4:43).

The kingdom of God is a locality where God rules, where his will is done. That locality can be in this world or out of it; it can be in the human heart, a home, a group of people, and a society, even a judicial or political chamber. Jesus said his kingdom was not of this world. He told his disciples the kingdom was in their hearts and to tell others it was not far from them. He instructed his disciples to seek it first and everything important would fall into place. He declared his missional intent from his hometown synagogue, and he sent his disciples to tell others about it. Peter preached about the kingdom at Pentecost, Philip taught it, and Paul was teaching it right to the end.[1] He said that the gospel of the kingdom would need to be preached throughout the whole world before the end would come (see Matthew 24:14 4). And when the end would come, it really was a beginning.

This is where the gospel of the kingdom shines, because it opens up new possibilities. Jesus taught us to pray, "Thy kingdom come. Thy will be done in earth, as it is in heaven" (Matthew 6:10, kjv). The entire redemptive drama is about God reclaiming his own—his people, his world, his creation. If Jesus didn't think the resurrection and restoration of the material world was important, he would have left his banged-up body in the grave. But he didn't. His restored body, with the same hands and feet, the same hair and eyes, the same wrinkles, aches, and pains of a thirty-three-year-old man, tells us that the material world was to be part of the restoration. It also says something about the application of the gospel to social ills, to the need for justice, the care of the environment, and the healing of lands and peoples. What does "God's will be done on earth as in heaven" mean? It means the whole gospel for the whole world. The full force of the gospel is that followers of Jesus are transformed in their spirits; they are reborn people set on their way by a new life. They are driven by the Spirit of God to make the world right. Those same people become Jesus to the world around them, feeding the hungry, saving the children, healing the sick, assisting the poor, and doing it in the name and power of the living Christ. The gospel of the kingdom is not only about saving souls; it is about those saved souls changing and caring for their world. As Dallas Willard teaches, the reborn spirit works its way through the mind, then the body, then through a person's social world.[2]

A healthy spirituality is not a privatized spirituality. It does not fall prey to the dualism of believing that nothing can be done about the world until Jesus returns and that when he returns, the world will burn up, so there is no reason to value the earth or the non-Christians in it. The gospel of the kingdom values both the earth and every person living on it. This leads to Christ followers not being fatalistic regarding the care of the earth. It causes them to rethink what it means to be a steward of God's creation. It helps Christians see the value of other people apart from just their religious beliefs.

What kind of Christian does the gospel of the kingdom create? The kingdom concept broadens the definition of each person's world and purpose. It frees disciples to enter the world and to affect it through their own gifts, skills, and interest. I love the story of the young man standing alone in a church before the altar, juggling. He was offering his best to God. Most Christians still don't believe that painting a landscape is as holy as preaching a sermon. It is a stretch for many to think of painting a needy person's home as important as serving Communion. Wouldn't it be cool for the house painter to think of his painting clothes as vestments? The broadening gospel of the kingdom allows people to be creative and contribute in nontraditional ways to the story of God in their lives and in the human experience. It certainly does not preclude all the tried-and-true traditional expressions: teaching, preaching, verbal witness. We must have it all. The gospel of the kingdom not only promises life after death, it also believes in life before death, in overcoming evil with good. This requires us to find our niche in the larger story of God and his redemptive work.

The Same Gospel

Of course, there are more "gospels" than the five I have proposed. Should we try to define them, debate their validity, and if so why? Is there just one gospel and what makes this one special or better? Without some way of connecting the church's well-being to the gospel of the kingdom, this exercise can be nothing more than an expedition to nowhere.

I believe that the gospel of the kingdom is what Jesus, Paul, Peter, and the early church believed and taught. Take a slice out of Jesus' teaching, and it is evident that the gospel of the kingdom and the gospel of eternal life through faith in Christ are the same. In Mark 10, Jesus' interaction with the rich young man indicates that faith and following Jesus are necessary to "eternal life." Jesus was explaining faith to the young man in a way that he could understand and where faith would be found real in the man's obedience. Later he told his disciples, "How hard it is for the rich to enter the Kingdom of God!" (Mark 10:23). Jesus taught Nicodemus that in order to see or enter the kingdom of God, he had to be born from above, from the Spirit (see John 3:3).

According to Simon Gathercole, Paul and the Synoptic writers had these three points of agreement:

> First, that Jesus was the promised Messianic King and Son of God come to earth as a servant in human form (Romans 1:3, 4; Philippians 4:4ff). Second, by his death and resurrection, Jesus atoned for our sin and secured our justification by grace, not by our works (1 Corinthians 15:3ff). Third, on the cross Jesus broke the dominion of sin and evil over us (Colossians 2:13-15) and at his return he will complete what he began by the renewal of the entire material creation and the resurrection of our bodies (Romans 8:18ff). Gathercole then traces these same three aspects in the Synoptic' teaching that Jesus, the Messiah, is the divine Son of God (Mark 1:1) who died as a substitutionary ransom for the many (Mark 10:45) who has conquered the demonic present age with its sin and evil (Mark 1:14-2:10) and will return to regenerate the material world (Matthew 19:28).

Tim Keller summarizes Gathercole's description of the gospel this way: "Through the person and work of Jesus Christ, God fully accomplishes salvation for us, rescuing us from judgment for sin into fellowship with him, and then restores the creation in which we can enjoy our new life together with him forever."[3]

So here's what you might say to a person about how to become a Christian:

> God created the world we all wanted, but our self-will and rebellion caused it to fall apart. Jesus came to show us the way. He spoke to injustice by becoming a victim of it through his crucifixion. He took the penalty for our sin, but he rose from the dead and provided a way for us to restore our relationship to God and see the restoration of the creation. He calls on us to believe in him, to follow him. When we join him as his disciples, we are to affect the world though his life in us. Our role is to support him in whatever he asks and our prayer "Thy will be done on earth as it is in heaven" then will be answered.

This is the gospel of the kingdom.

The Gospel of the Kingdom at Work

What has our inattention to this gospel and to spiritual formation cost us? Numerically this is a hard question to answer. To determine what might have been is nearly impossible. Many have made a career from speaking and writing about the church in crisis, and this career will always be there for the taking because the church is perpetually in need. G. K. Chesterton found humor in prognostication. He wrote,

> One of the games to which (the human race) is most attached is called "Keep tomorrow dark," and which is also named "Cheat the prophet." The players listen very carefully and respectfully to all that clever men have to say about what is to happen in the next generation. The players then wait until all the clever men are dead, and bury them nicely. They then go and do something else.[4]

That being said, the best way I know to answer the question of what our inattention has cost us is to compare the contemporary church with the early church. Here's a quick overview of the work of the first-century church.

Solid research shows the church to be at around ten thousand at the end of the first century. One tends to forget the vulgarities of church life. Three thousand men came to faith and were baptized on Pentecost, but many went home and some dropped out. The church developed a smaller core community. The descriptions of growth in the book of Acts are not specific, but taken with the parable of the sower, those who remained faithful were in the minority.[5] Still, the church grew exponentially until it peaked with regard to population at around 33,882,008 in 350 AD, or 56.5 percent of the Roman world.[6]

It would be difficult to imagine a greater success for the church than the Roman world accepting Christianity because it was a majority. The church grew at a rate of 40 percent per decade during the first four centuries. This percentage allows for the normal process of conversion and for Christianity being passed on to the next generation. Constantine's conversion can be best explained as a political response to the powerful wave of the Christian reality. Augustine, who lived in the 400s, claimed that the church's growth was a result of miracles.

The greatest miracle, however, was the response of Christians to persecution and to plagues and the treatment of women and children. The church didn't sponsor organized evangelistic meetings to speak of; Christians impacted the world through their deeds. I don't mean to imply that contemporary churches shouldn't organize outreach. Modern life in the West requires some stimulus to awaken us from the spiritual slumber. I mean to say that urban life in ancient cities was crowded, characterized by sewage in the streets, which led to polluted drinking water. As Rodney Stark writes, "Greco-Roman cities must have been smothered in flies, mosquitoes, and other insects that flourish where there was much stagnant water and exposed filth. And, like bad odors, insets are very democratic."[7] This, of course, led to illness and plagues, which opened the door wide for the church. One reason Jesus and the apostles healed so many was the sheer volume of human need.

One of the reasons for the rise of the faith was the church's protection of human life. The early church was against infanticide, which was routinely practiced in the Greco-Roman world, especially against girls. The sad result of such a practice was a significant shortage of females. The church was also against abortion; Christians took care of orphans and widows in a culture that discarded them. And most dramatic of all, they stayed in the cities and nursed the sick, even during plagues. The percentage of Christians who died of epidemics was significantly less because Christians nursed their sick. Simple sanitation saved many lives, and the fact that Christians didn't flee to the countryside in order to save themselves was a powerful demonstration of their love.

The Kingdom Affect

This was Christian character at work, and it's what we might call "the kingdom affect." The church didn't have dedicated buildings during this period; the early Christians didn't become famous or rich for filling buildings or serving others. As one wise sage proposed, "The church was at its best when it had the least." I suspect that it wasn't because these early Christians had extended quiet times or read many books or kept journals. Most of them were illiterate; they simply allowed the community of Christ to set the standard. They listened to the truth of the Word of God and allowed the faith communities in which they lived to form them.

The kingdom affect was the natural response of these early Christians to the needs around them. Add to this the church's martyrs and their willingness to sacrifice their lives for the truth and you have a powerful movement that could not be stopped. The word *martyr* means to be a witness. "Martyrs are the most credible exponents of the value of religion, and this is especially true if there is a voluntary aspect to their martyrdom."[8] Nothing could match martyrdom in a head-to-head match for credibility.

Consider the martyrdom of James, Paul, and Peter. They went to their deaths with joy and great courage. Contrary to common opinion, few ordinary Christians were killed by the Romans. The vast majority were leaders, bishops, and the famous. They faced death bravely; they were wonderful examples of the sacrificial life. They didn't get rich, they were not paid, and they didn't take advantage of their celebrity. John Wycliffe was put on trial and William Tyndale was executed because they sought to translate the Bible into English. They both stood strong in the face of death. One might remember reading about Ignatius, the bishop of Antioch, as he traveled to Rome in anticipation of his own martyrdom. He wrote ahead to request that no Roman citizen of influence intervene to get him clemency.[9] Tradition has it that Peter, Polycarp, and even Paul also could have negotiated their way out of being killed, but they thought it beneath them and their example in Christ to do so. There was a resolve among the faithful. They went ahead, whether it was nursing the sick and knowing they would die as a result, or going to a certain area to be killed for sport, like Ignatius.

The kingdom affect is still going on in much of the world. More people are killed today than ever before because they are Christian. That is partly because there are more than one billion Christians and many live under tyranny. But we still see Christians with great pluck who live in the same horrid conditions that many early believers did. Where those same conditions exist, Christians today behave much as they did in the first three centuries. Of course, there are superficial and selfish disciples who run for the hills, who deny they are Christians and ignore those in need. It often seems that in such cases, the life of Christ has not found its way from their heads to their legs. This would be in the tradition of the pre-Pentecost eleven, such as Peter swearing at the servant girl in the courtyard of Caiaphas. Even bishops recanted under duress, but most stayed true. The faithful are still the faithful.

The Existing Kingdom Affect in the West

The church in the West has responded in many good ways to the needs in the world: building hospitals, providing on-the-ground health care and emergency services such as the Red Cross. A healthy new trend is short-term mission trips, especially for teens, which help them learn about the world and that something can be done about problems. There are now global initiatives that are attempting to address the vast nature of the crisis: to bring clean water where there is none, to combat government corruption, to fight for freedom of religion and speech along with the treatment of malaria and related disease. These global missions are being conducted primarily through Western philanthropy. The vast majority of money and personnel comes from the contemporary Western church.

However, the kingdom affect has been lost in the West, in first-world nations. A Western Christian can go days, even months, without encountering needs that are difficult to ignore. Needs are not around us in a tactile way. We drive through the need in our air-conditioned cars with the windows up and the music playing. We see the need on the evening news or read about it in newspapers and magazines. It is tough to understand the need or feel it when we are insulated from it. Most affluent people are not responsible for these barriers, nor should they feel guilty about it. They are just our reality.

Still, if it wants to affect the world like the Christians in the early church, the contemporary church in the first world has to tear down some barriers.

The first barrier that needs to be eradicated is the privatization of the spiritual life. The mission of this book is limited, but I believe the church needs to see that a spirituality that addresses only personal status with God, forgiven or not forgiven, is only half of the story. The purpose of the inner life is to make for a powerful outer life. While some may propose that a good inner life is enough, that it doesn't need to be lived out in public, this is not what Christ taught. There is a tendency among our more contemplative brothers and sisters to detach practice of the inner life from any logical effect. The Sermon on the Mount should put such a notion to rest.

The mission of the church has been limited to the "spiritual mission" of getting souls saved. Is there anything more important than that? No, there isn't, but what is meant by salvation? Salvation is a journey that begins with entrance into a relationship with God. It is about the *whole person*, not just the soul. It is about growing and being shaped into the image of Christ in this present life, and it is about the future life. There is also real life to be lived here and now. Not only the life after death, but life before death. More precisely, eternal life before death. Salvation is about the reign of the kingdom of God.

The kingdom exists when the life of God is within us, when his presence is evident. We might even say it would need to be his active presence. It is within us and travels with us, wherever we go. (It also has a futuristic dimension that is not a part of this discussion.) So how can the life of Christ that is being lived and shaped in me cause me to have the same affect on others that the early Christians had? How can the life of Christ in me cause a resurgence of the faith in the West instead of the steady decline that is now the case?

The answer addresses the second barrier the contemporary church must tear down: the lack of good teaching on the kingdom. The kingdom is foreign to our natural thinking. Americans in particular have no place in their brains for such an idea to lodge. It is an antiquated concept. It doesn't seem real. The idea of church is much easier to grasp.

Pastors commonly teach that all God's activity on this earth is mediated through the local church. This has led to the teaching that the highest priority for Christians is to get the world to go to church. As a result, all the money, personnel, and attention are focused on the Sunday-gathered church. While I believe that what happens on Sunday is every bit as important as what happens the others six days of the week, Scripture never commands non-Christians to go to church. We have wasted a lot of time, money, and resources attempting to convince them they should. This accounts for huge neon signs that say such things as "Come Grow with Us," or "Wednesday Night Is Family Night," or "Sermon Series, 'The End of the World,' Be There!"

This all seems so ineffectual, even silly. The church meets in order to go to the world, and that world can be called the harvest field. To borrow one of Jesus' images, the church goes out to live as wheat among tares. We are so closely connected to others that only God's wisdom and knowledge can separate the two. I have always been intrigued by Malcolm Muggeridge's little book *A Third Testament*. It studies the lives and teaching of Augustine, Blaise Pascal, William Blake, Søren Kierkegaard, Theodore Dostoevsky, Leo Tolstoy, and Dietrich Bonhoeffer. Muggeridge posits that all seven are God's spies, posted in actual or potential enemy-occupied territory, the enemy being, in this particular case, the Devil. Muggeridge thought of these men as clandestine infiltrators that would organize sabotage in preparation for the coming invasion. Augustine and Bonhoeffer easily would have been separated as wheat from among the tares, but others would have been difficult to define as wheat. For example, Dostoevsky and Tolstoy. Their lives were filled with addiction and all the extremes that go with it. A footnote to history is that Tolstoy's private farm idea was what inspired Gandhi's attempt to live in a self-sufficient society in western India. Both Tolstoy and Gandhi sensed they had found the secret to harmony in the Sermon on the Mount. Muggeridge contends that the two Russians' works kept the gospel alive in Russia for a hundred years. Impact is often subtle, indirect, or even seminal until it has had time to grow into a force.

So the kingdom affect is how our personal spirituality, which is never meant to be private, affects the various parts of the world. The kingdom is our family, our places of work, public schools, neighborhoods, the entertainment industry, government institutions, politics, media, literature, universities, and, of course, our local church. The church is an outpost in the larger world of the kingdom. It must be said that the church is not the kingdom but only a part of it. The real action is Monday through Saturday, when Christians then behave in ways natural for the spiritually mature, and the result is impact. The disciple does what a disciple's character dictates. He or she meets needs, lives the truth, and stands up for the weak and disenfranchised. On this last point, Bonhoeffer was clear: Unless the church stands between the oppressed and the oppressor, it is not being the church.

Until the last hundred years, most of the world was in survival mode. There was not a lot of time for philosophical reflection, the pursuit of hobbies, or anxiety over the many choices of how we might spend our time and money. Of course, there has always been the privileged, the aristocrats, the royals, the political leaders, and the academic community who have pursued the arts. But for the common person, survival was the order of the day. For the contemporary Christian, recognizing and meeting needs is subtler; it requires discernment to know when to speak and when to act. The principle is the same, however. Early Christians risked their lives to nurse the sick because it was a value lived out in the faith community. We need to teach by example this discernment and service to others in the context and support of community. Most of us would fail miserably to do the things we sense we should unless we were taught and supported by others.

Because the American church has neglected intentional spiritual formation, most Christians do not have the kind of witness that early Christians had. This lack has led to a serious decline in our influence and credibility. We live in a media age; a circus of strange and extreme characters dominates the Christian airwaves and has brought much shame to the church. The media has done to the church what the church has done to the general culture. First, we felt superior to the "world" because of our conviction that we have the truth. Second, we separated ourselves from culture in the worst possible way. We created Christian versions of the Boy Scouts, schools, and an assortment of clubs. But in practice, we didn't leave behind bitterness, anger, lust, materialism, gossip, and a love for the "flesh." We created a straw man of unbelievers, making them the enemy. Finally, we have either judged unbelievers through accusatory preaching or ignored them through separation.

Yes, there are quality Christian preachers on television, but then again some of them pay themselves shameful amounts of money and live as celebrities. As I pointed out in the previous chapter, many teach that wealth is a sign of God's blessing. They don't seem to see the irony of such ministries always being in need of money. My point is that the general public just laughs and sees no spiritual reality they can respect. This may not be a fair analysis to some, but I contend that the most famous of the famous have been corrupted by the culture. Because the most luminous spiritual leaders in our culture don't seem to make intentional discipleship a priority, it's not a high priority for the church in general. Our leaders are impatient people driven to success—nickels and noses, bodies and bucks, book sales, and so on. Even the hardworking parish priest or pastor fights the battle every day between serving Christ and living for others and the push to make his church grow in order to have a bigger ministry. It is tough not to get caught up in the rush to live in the fast lane of spirituality. The forces of culture are confusing. On one hand, there is great support for tolerance and equality in race and gender. But on the other, truth as a category has collapsed, so the reasons why we should show grace and dignity to our fellow human beings have disappeared. People in general are still deeply moved by stories of sacrifice and bravery, yet they have fewer reasons to live sacrificial lives.

What has our inattention to the gospel of the kingdom cost us? It is a two-edged sword that has done injury to our cause. We have lowered the cost on what it means to follow Christ and, as a result, it is less valued. The sword's other edge is that because it is less valued, we are less willing to make it a central part of life.

While it's common to think that when you ask for more commitment, people flee, studies have shown the exact opposite. The truth is, increased expectations for membership increase participation and make joining the organization attractive to outsiders.[10] When the price is high, so are the rewards.

The church has grown significantly in the United States over the last three hundred years. In fact, that is an understatement. It has shaped our culture; it created our institutions; it formed us as a nation. Honest historians would have to give it credit for our system of justice and the basis for morality, without which democracy cannot function. But we are now in the afterglow of such a powerful showing. The American church is on the wane and is seriously compromised.

Like every generation, we have a duty to turn it around, to do the things that could change our trajectory. I contend that the starting point is a renewed interest and commitment on the part of Christian leaders to the slow, ordinary work of forming people in Christ, so I've devoted most of the chapters in this book to a discussion of what this means. I'm not advocating that we stop doing at the expense of being, nor that we shut down our mission's projects or stop building hospitals, feeding the hungry, and loving the world in word and deed. I wrote this book to encourage Christians to intentionally pursue spiritual formation and to take on the image of Christ—to pursue a life of humility, submission, obedience, and sacrifice. I think Dallas Willard says it best:

> Widespread transformation of character through wisely disciplined discipleship to Christ can transform our world. It can disarm the structural evils that have always dominated humankind and now threaten to destroy the world.[11]

While statistics show a shrinking church in the United States, they also show a growing church in the Southern Hemisphere. As historian Philip Jenkins points out at the end of his important work *The Next Christendom*, "Christianity is never as weak as it appears, nor as strong as it appears. And whether we look backward or forward in history, we can see that time and again, Christianity demonstrates a breathtaking ability to transform weakness into strength."[12]

Reflections

People of faith are yearning for something stronger, deeper. They want an unsentimental faith that is up to the challenge of real life. But this kind of faith comes from that kind of gospel—a gospel where faith is real in obedience, a gospel where grace is active not passive, a gospel that equates following Jesus as believing in Jesus. This kind of gospel sees the world as a place we live among all peoples and sees Christians as those who take on the character of the gospel, who bring humility, submission, obedience, and sacrifice to those who need it. This gospel has a payoff and a penalty; otherwise the whole thing doesn't matter that much.

CHAPTER 3

A Messy, Lifelong Journey

When we first became Christians, most of us had a naïve vision of our religious future. It looked something like this: Angelic choirs would sing as we, undistracted by thoughts of malice or thirst for power, faithfully and naturally served Christ all our days. We assumed that with a few more Bible studies and training in resistance, temptation would get easier to handle. We figured our prayer life would become as natural as eating or sleeping, and the desire for material things would be brought into submission. We had the idyllic hope that spiritual growth would be intense for an initial period but that as we matured we would coast or float above the fray.

Life takes these naïve impressions and shatters them on the hard rocks of reality. Here's a case in point. Several years ago I was reading the Saturday paper when my hand froze halfway to my coffee cup. There it was in the overnight crime report, the name of one of my most faithful parishioners: Jack, a seventy-five-year-old Sunday school teacher. He had been arrested the previous night for soliciting a prostitute. I am not sure what was more shocking: that a seventy-five-year-old was trolling for prostitutes or that a well-read, seasoned follower of Christ was doing so. Jack usually started the day reading the Scriptures and praying with his wife. He devoted many hours to listening to Christian radio and reading books on the Christian life. His hobby was reading systematic theology. A Sunday didn't go by that he wouldn't share some spiritual jewel with me from his studies. Jack was practicing the spiritual disciplines; he was a man of prayer. Yet he had also been driving around at night with a cigarette hanging out of his mouth and had pulled up to the curb in his rattletrap car and talked dirty with the girls. He never got out of the car, but the female police officer arrested him.

It is worth noting that it is not uncommon for a person who practices the right activities to do so and live a double life. Men in particular are able to partition off secret worlds that they make themselves believe are not real or don't really count. They can live in an "Andy of Mayberry" world, but if given the opportunity and with the thought that they would not be caught, they would bed Aunt Be. So they go off and do their dark deeds, then reenter their normal lives. They feel safe when their wife or other family members treat them normally. *Whew, got away with it again.*

Over the next year, two other members of the church joined Jack in the infamy that goes with allowing your libido to reign. They were arrested in the same area of town for the same reason. The first was a forty-five-year-old married man, the other an eighteen-year-old who worked with the junior high boys. All of these men were serious Christians but malformed. They'd had a wrong understanding of grace and what constitutes true spirituality.

Three men in different stages of life, each desperate in his own way. Something in them permitted them to step over the line. It is a fair question to ask, "Why did they do this?" It isn't so much a mystery that a Christian man will get caught up in lust, but these serious Christians made up lies in order to leave home, get into their cars, drive to a particular part of town, and roll down their car windows to talk with prostitutes. The two younger men had seen what had happened to Jack. They were in church when he confessed. He repented and changed, and the years he had left were his happiest. But he paid a high price socially. He endured the shame that came with his public humiliation and the unforgiveness of some members who were disgusted with his behavior. These two men had heard the whispers in the corridors, the outright disgust in the coffee shops. Yet something very strong within pushed them on. Why did this happen?

A few conventional causes would be an unhappy home life, an addiction to pornography, and the habit of giving in to impulse. The seventy-five-year-old was trying to bring back the past, the eighteen-year-old was seeking the future, the forty-five-year-old was trying to break the boredom. But psychological reasons fall short in explaining why these men did not live up to their own ideas of good. They knew that what they were doing was wrong. That is why they chose the darkness as the proper setting to explore what gibbered within. The below-the-line issues in a person's life that lead to hiding and acting out are often left untouched in a non-discipleship religious environment.

The Thin Veil

A fine line separates good from evil. In an instant, we cross it, sometimes suddenly with intense emotion and at other times deliberately, after thoughtful reflection. Being formed into the image of Christ is a lifelong journey. It's naïve to think that being spiritually formed will eliminate primal lust. No matter our age—whether seventy-five, forty-five, or eighteen—it doesn't matter. We must always be on guard against what Paul calls "the flesh." The flesh is crouching at the door (see Genesis 4:7) and will pounce without warning because it never improves. No matter how far you get, disaster is always just a poor decision away.

Can a person with highly formed Christlikeness within suddenly fail in a disastrous way? Yes, it can and does happen. But I would claim that it would be an event rather than a pattern. The fruit of longevity in spiritual formation leading to Christian character makes such disaster less likely. This entire cycle can be broken, even stopped, by practicing the basic principles of discipleship: honesty, vulnerability, and submission. It also means a quicker recovery and restart on the right path.

The bad news is that the veil does not thicken over time. There is still that putrid truth that if I could get away with acting out in my body what my mind wants to do, I probably would. This may be the darker side, but there are also letdowns in other areas of character. Human development is not fixed; it can regress. For instance, older people tend to become more judgmental and sometimes mean. Who hasn't been on the receiving end or been a witness to a senior citizen's wrath while in line at the store? Some of them call the police when a parked car is hanging more than one foot onto their driveway or when the party next door is a bit too loud. In most cases, in their earlier life they never would have considered complaining. I think this is a habit of fear that grips us as we age — the fear that the young will dominate our lives, that our opinions are no longer wanted, that our rights will be neglected. As our bodies grow weak and our influence wanes, it is easy to become a victim.

This is why we need instruction and to be involved in a community of supportive, trustworthy people our whole life long. These needs never go away. There is nothing quite as sweet as an older person who is at peace, who is content and radiates joy. Whether we become a fearful or content older person is largely dependent on the habits we formed in life and on the influence of those who surround us. The veil remains thin, but the development of good habits over time makes it much less likely that we will slip through to the other side.

The Myth of Moral Advancement

The late Russian novelist and activist Alexander Solzhenitsyn famously said the line between good and evil runs through the center of people's hearts. There are some who believe that to be anachronistic, a pre-Enlightenment notion. The Enlightenment was a movement that placed humankind and reason at the center of life. In order for humanity and our capabilities to be central, God had to be moved out.

One of the most egregious examples occurred in the French Revolution when Norte Dame ceased to be a church and was renamed the Temple of Reason. The idea behind the Enlightenment was that humankind could advance morally thorough science and reason. No doubt people have advanced through science and reason. It is much better to have surgery with aesthesia than a shot of Jack Daniels and a bullet to bite. But science has severe limitations as to its ability to improve a person's basic nature. It can only observe the human condition and comment on it or change it physically. It has no explanation as to how the world began, why people are moral, the origins of conscience, love, or any human emotion. Science can locate the speech center in the brain, but can it answer why we speak, laugh, or cry?

Today we are undergoing a resurgence of belief in science and reason as a superior way to look at the world. This renaissance has come primarily though the new atheism proposed by Sam Harris, Dennis Dennett, Richard Dawkins, and Christopher Hitchens. It is militant and accompanied by a great deal of anger and hubris. Their anger is directed at a God who has broken their moral code. Hitchens likes to cite that humankind in its present manifestation has been around for a hundred thousand years. He scoffs at a God who would allow his children to struggle in a "survival of the fittest" world for 98,000 of those years and then capriciously send his "savior-son" two thousand years ago. Hitchens never does cite the source of his own moral code or how one knows good from evil. The irony of this movement is that its proponents believe that the world would be a kinder and better place without religion. There is an element of truth to this in that much of the religion in the world could be done without, especially the more toxic forms. But to the new atheists, *toxic* means people of conviction and any religion that makes exclusive truth claims. They don't like to mention the atheism of Stalin, Mao, Hitler, or Pol Pot, all of whom accounted for the death of a hundred million in the twentieth century. That is the Social Darwinism they so much admire: the survival of the fittest, the elimination of the weak, a brave new world where morality has no reason to exist. It is Nietzsche's Superman, the will to power, a world beyond good and evil.

Nietzsche's Superman concept was the philosophy championed by

Adolf Hitler. One can picture the highly cultured, smart, well-educated lovers of art, science, and history sitting in a drawing room somewhere in Berlin, smoking cigars, sipping the best brandy, and listening to Wagner. They were testaments to moral improvement through education and science—Social Darwinism gone amuck. They didn't know for certain that the world would be a better place without belief in God; they just chose to believe it, despite powerful evidence to the contrary. (One can't help but be reminded of Pascal's Wager. He reasoned if a person bet his or her life that there is a God, that there is a final accounting, and that we end up either in heaven or hell, and was wrong, nothing lost, nothing gained. But if that person was right, he or she gained eternal life. If a person bet his or her life that there is no God or final accounting, and was wrong, then eternity in hell would be that individual's lot, and there is much to lose.)

The idea that humanity is morally evolving should have died after World War I. Europeans realized after 1918 that the war was much like a circular firing squad. In World War I, 8.5 million soldiers were killed along with 10 million civilians. World War II killed 60 million people. John Keegan estimates another 50 million have died in various conflicts.[1] Knowledge did not set us free; reality ripped the heart out of the Enlightenment. Many have proposed that the evolutionary process joined to equal rights and better education will change the heart of humans. The entire idea is a failed one; anyone who takes an honest look at the evidence would be required to reject it. In more recent days, the orgy of greed seen on Wall Street makes the case. Politicians don't like to cast blame on the average citizen, but this situation would not have happened without the unbridled lust of the American public.

The Only Hope for Change of Character

The only hope for change of character, and for a revolutionary change of a society, comes from within. It is my contention that this change will not come from better education or from reading great books or from eating a better diet and having medical care. All of those things can improve our lives, but they can't change our inner person. That can be done only through God entering us and our working with him to transform us. I would propose that it is possible that a properly formed disciple could desire *not to desire* things that displease God.

Servant or Slave?

Paul used the term *flesh* thirty-four times. Most of the time, he was referring to that part of us that is both material and immaterial and at war against God. Sometimes he used *flesh* to mean the body, other times to mean futile human effort. Then there is *flesh* as the enemy of God.[2] One of the most important examples is when Paul explained the war between the works of the flesh and the fruit of the Spirit (see Galatians 5:16-17). Another is when he dressed down the Corinthians and accused them of behaving as people of the flesh (see 1 Corinthians 3:1-3). The evidence was jealousy and strife. (Whenever you read the words *flesh*, *selfish desires*, or a similar English translation of the Greek word *sarx*, context determines its meaning.)

It is obvious that the flesh is fallen and that the human body is part of that fall, since the body decays and dies. Because of this, some Christians make the error of not valuing the body as a part of our spiritual person. They reason that at death this old body goes away and we get a new glorified body. However, although the flesh includes the body, the body is not all bad. We must understand that it is the resource to deliver the life of Christ to others. Left to itself, the body is a tool of the fallen nature and a source of sin. But to treat the body as identical with our fallen nature has its problems. George Fox, who founded the Quakers, pointed them out.

> These professors said that the outward body was the body of death and sin. I showed them their mistake in that also; for Adam and Eve had each of them an outward body, before the

body of death and sin got into them; and that man and woman will have bodies when the body of sin and death is put off again; when they are renewed up into the image of God again by Jesus Christ, which they were in before the fall.[3]

So when Paul exhorted us to the "putting off of the sinful nature" (Colossians 2:11, NIV) or to "have crucified the sinful nature with its passions and desires" (Galatians 5:24, NIV), he did not recommend destroying the entire body; that is suicide. But he did recommend a course of action in the power of Christ. What Paul meant is crucial. He was saying that either the body can be our servant or we can be its slave. We become the body's slave when we trust in it rather than in God. This is so easy to do because we can create immediate results that give us pleasure. Our body has many abilities; at its worst, it is dedicated to the trilogy of the lust of the flesh, the lust of the eyes, and the pride of life, which John warns us are not of the Father but of this world (see 1 John 2:16). There is nothing wrong with many desires of the flesh when the flesh is a disciplined, Spirit-filled body. There certainly is nothing bad in the use of one's eyes or in taking pride in your person and work. Again, the context means everything. Who or what is in charge? At its best, our body goes into training so it will do what it should and willingly get on the altar of life as a living sacrifice (see Romans 12:1).

The human body controlled and trained by the Spirit of God is our primary tool to deliver the reality of Christ to the world. The role of spiritual exercises is to mold and shape us so we are able to fulfill our mission. So when I say that the flesh never improves, I mean that our fallen nature will always be with us. But that doesn't mean it has to be in control. The battle is a spiritual one, but when the body is in service to Christ, its ugly passions and desires are diminished.

Competing Desires

Paul introduced facts into the human experience in order to knock down the subjectivism that was ruining the early church. Subjectivism is doing the same in the church today. People who are normally right-thinking tend to lose their way when it comes to desire and religious behavior. They reason, *I know that at work I must conduct myself a certain way and engage in various duties to succeed. In order to do so, I must deny my desire to goof off, cheat, and engage in other immoral deeds.* However, some of these folks take a different position when asked about desire in the religious realm. They will propose that religious feeling is required for religious conduct. They tell themselves, *If I don't want to do something that God's Word tells me I should do, it would be wrong for me to do it until I can do it wholeheartedly.* The truth is, it's normal for us to have competing desires. The desires of the "flesh" are opposed to the Spirit and will of God. Therefore, the "works of the flesh" must be resisted; it is not open to debate. John Calvin said, "The ruin of a man is to obey himself."[4] This would imply that giving in to the desires of the flesh would ruin a person's life. The better option is to train your body so that it and its desires become your servant (see 1 Corinthians 9:24-27).[5] The new life in Christ in us does mature, and I believe that it can take dominance, but it is a wrestling match, and the opponent can score points.[6]

That being said, there are many Christians for whom spiritual maturity is a far-off fantasy. I don't think most people aspire to spiritual maturity because it is too general and conceptual. Instead, they have goals that are precise and rooted in immediate need, such as the goal to control their temper or to forgive a friend.

Many Christians are taught that after a time of basic training, the Christian experience becomes more natural, the dangers less prominent. That is why there is disillusionment and confusion as to why one stops making progress and why more heinous sins continue to have a grip on us. The new challenges of every season of life become setbacks and causes for self-condemnation. We think that we shouldn't be feeling this or doing that. The truth is that throughout our life, our primary enemy is self, the desire to please self and to interpret life through our own limited perspective. The goal of Christlikeness is to live to please

God, to interpret life through his perspective, and to live for others.

But if we stop exercising spiritually, we can regress. There is an old saying, "What do you have to do to get out of shape?" The answer is, "Nothing."

The Ease of Spiritual Regression

Thirty years ago I started to exercise. I had taken five years off after my basketball days and faithfully gained ten pounds a year. Fifty pounds overweight, I looked in the mirror and didn't like my reality. I started running and existing on 1500 calories a day. Eight months later, I was fifty-five pounds lighter and was having difficulty eating enough to stop the weight loss.

Over the last three decades, I have been fairly good. I still exercise every other day, I eat right 70 percent of the time, but I have gained back around twenty pounds. How did that happen? My metabolism slowed, certain medications have slowed me down and make it harder to exercise at full tilt, and I have started eating more desserts. And then there are the aches and pains. They come without warning or explanation; they attack me when I am asleep, eating breakfast, or simply sunning myself (oh, can't do that—skin cancer!). Recently I read a book that recommended I exercise six days a week, acquire a heart monitor, and lift weights. Doesn't this author realize I had a double-hernia operation last year from lifting a case of Coke?

I realized that I had been giving in to age and that I needed to attack it. I had regressed via ease. Now I am going to war against aging, decay, and negativity. (If you want motivation, visit a nursing home.) I think of exercise as a stewardship issue. Regardless of how long God gives me, I want to be as useful as possible. I don't believe in Christian fatalism, which believes we can play no part in our health or quality of life. It may be true that the length of our days is already determined, but the quality of those days is not. To be that passive is an absurdity. There seems to be much evidence that how we take care of ourselves lengthens our days. I suppose that if you must, you can posit that God wills some people to exercise, eat right, and live longer and that it is part of his sovereignty, but few want to talk about this.

We are talking about regression, and I must confess that some of the same regression has take place in my spiritual life. Many of us begin to live on yesterday's manna, our biblical knowledge base. We can do this for a time because a good spiritual track record serves us well. But at some point, going soft on planned prayer, Bible reading, and working on service projects with like-minded disciples creates a distance from Christ and his heart for others.

Spiritual regression is a bit different than the danger of a sudden fall through the thin veil. Regression is gradual; it is a product of a negative pattern. A positive pattern requires intention and discipline and usually the help of friends. A negative pattern most often is characterized by ease. It requires a loss of focus, neglect of discipline, and withdrawal from helpful friends. Structure and accountability empower people, enabling them to practice what makes them successful. Ease comes naturally; you don't need to practice it. You just drift into it. Some would call ease our default position, the one to which we naturally return when we stop short of forming a new habit.

That was the case with Samuel Johnson, who is considered second only to William Shakespeare as a literary genius in British history. He was a man of prodigious intellect; he is most famous for his version of the English dictionary, which established the English language as a world-class language. Many have said that Shakespeare had the theater, Christopher Wren had Saint Paul's Cathedral, and Johnson had the English language. He was a large man with highly quirky mannerisms, today called Tourette syndrome. Two words were used of him and they dominated his life: *indolence* and *melancholia*. Today we would use *laziness* and *depression*. Like many high-strung wunderkinds, Johnson would wallow in his own self-indulgences for months without working and then burst forth with a remarkable string of superhuman accomplishment. He planned to spend three years on the English dictionary; it took ten years of torturous self-loathing. Sometimes months of sloth and debauchery would pass without a word being penned, as this description shows:

> He is a very large man, and was dressed in a dirty brown coat and waistcoat, with breeches that were brown also (though they had been crimson), and an old black wig: his shirt collar and sleeves were unbuttoned; his stockings were down about his feet, which had on them, by way of slippers, an old pair of shoes. It was one o'clock in the afternoon and Johnson has just got up from bed: He seldom goes to bed till near two in the morning.[7]

Johnson was also a man of faith. He prayed. He wrote many wonderful prayers and rewrote prayer books. And he struggled greatly with his dark side. He was a man of resolution; he would promise himself that in a particular year he would improve his ways—that he wouldn't drink as much, spend as much time in pubs entertaining his friends and foes. He hated how much pleasure he got from revelry and how much torture his work had become. Johnson often regressed, not just slightly like most people. He would free-fall, like a man falling off a building. Story after story he would drop before hitting bottom. But like most genius prima donnas, he had friends and patrons to help him along.

His life was so much less than it could have been, at least that is what most of us would conclude. Some might say he was all that he could have been, given what he was, but I refuse to bow at the altar of this reality. As a Christian, I must hold to the idea of sanctification. Johnson and everyone wandering this planet, myself included, are called to something better.

Johnson is a larger-than-life example of the human condition. On a much smaller screen, we live and struggle, but with just as important results. So many of us never train to develop the new habits necessary to our success. But it is even more alarming to witness the atrophy of a positive habit already formed.

It is generally believed that arising early is a good habit. Most people report that the morning hours are their most productive. This is true of most adults over thirty who are not rock stars. It is alarming how a change in circumstances can see this positive pattern erode. Something as simple as a time change or a short illness can disrupt a desired habit. So you start slipping. Maybe a new medication makes it harder to get up, and you start getting up late three days a week, then five days, and then it becomes a habit to sleep in. You sleep more and then too much. Your sense of well-being declines and your productivity is reduced. As a result, you feel bad. All you did was allow ease to take control; your body became your master.

A Not-So-Easy Regression

Several years ago, I was flying from one city in Tajikistan to another. I had left Los Angeles two days earlier, just having learned that I had a hernia. My doctor had warned me that if it ruptured, and if I were not operated on within twelve hours, I would die. I imagined being taken to a Tajik hospital to be treated by a graduate of Aeroflot School of Medicine and Animal Husbandry. I tried to assure myself that with a bullet to bite, a shot of Jack Daniels, a pair of pliers, and bailing wire, I would be just fine.

A few minutes after landing in Tajikistan, I was trembling in a cold bed, trying to get some rest between flights. Turkish Air makes only two flights into Dushanbe, Tajikistan, a week. We arrived on the 3:20 flight Monday morning. It departs from there at 5:30 a.m. and doesn't return until Thursday. I lay shaking in the bed, praying the Jesus Prayer of the Eastern Orthodox Church *Jesus Christ, have mercy on me.* I was gripped by fear. I quoted, "Do not be anxious about anything, but in everything, by prayer and petition, with thanksgiving, present your requests to God. And the peace of God, which transcends all understanding, will guard your hearts and your minds in Christ

Jesus" (Philippians 4:6-7, NIV). I wanted the prayer to work, but I continued to shake. I even called a doctor back in the States to ask why I was shaking. My own diagnosis was fear and adrenaline. I castigated myself for being so stupid in making the trip. I had a primal urge to order my driver to take me back to the airport. I could still catch that 5:30, and who would blame me? Most people wouldn't have made the trip in the first place. Just then I heard the roar of jet engines as that lone plane disappeared into the early morning sky. I moaned, gritted my teeth, and stuffed my face into the pillow.

The next few days, I faithfully taught four hours a day. I never knew this before, but a hernia and public speaking do not go well together. The pain got worse as the days went by, and so did my anxiety. By force of will I made my presentations and fulfilled my mission. But I didn't enjoy it and couldn't wait to get out of there. It felt so good to lift off from that barren terrain and fly toward Istanbul, as though somehow I was safer or more protected by God. What a foolish man I had become.

I was on an airplane for the next twenty out of thirty hours until I returned home. I felt better in Istanbul, even better in New York, and absolutely giddy when we touched down at LAX. I told myself that I would get the hernia fixed in the next week or so and get on with my life.

It wasn't that simple. I scheduled the surgery, but then I developed some problems in my right leg. I feared that the long flight had caused a blood clot to form in my leg and that I was in danger of immediate disaster. You know, death. So I went to the emergency room and was tested for clots, but the tests proved negative. A few days later I was back at the same ER with the same complaint, but now I had a new swelling behind my right knee. The doctors wouldn't test me again for blood clots because they had confidence in the first test. But they X-rayed me in various places. I also had a CAT scan of my pelvis. The surgeon who ordered it called me while I still was in the ER. He lectured me with great confidence that I did not have a blood clot. After even more tests, the ER doctor came into my cubical and lectured me as well. There was no evidence that I had what I thought I had.

But no one could tell me what I had. I figured I needed to take charge of my health care, so I went to Urgent Care. The doctor there thought I might have a clot, but once again the tests came back negative. I went home happy but still skeptical. I couldn't sleep without a pill. So I went back to my own doctor. He ran more tests and rechecked me. That night I had pains in my leg, and it seemed to be getting worse. I was on the verge of going to the ER once more, but I thought they would throw me out. The next day I walked into my doctor's office without an appointment and found my doctor on his lunch break. He looked at me and said, "You look sick, toxic." He was stumped. We spent about an hour doing a few more checks, and he even asked a colleague in to examine me.

He finally closed his office door and sat down on one of those little stools on wheels doctors tend to use for examinations. I actually didn't know how bad I looked, but I had lost fifteen pounds and was in misery. I couldn't seem to get an answer as to why I had the problems. He told me to put off the hernia surgery until I was feeling better. I took a deep breath and told him I thought what was happening in my body was the product of more than thirty days of anxiety, stress, and not knowing what to do. I hate loose ends and this was a serious loose end. I couldn't control what was happening; I was afraid I would have to cancel my ministry schedule, which accounts for a good share of my income. And to add insult to injury, my back had seized up on me and I was in even more pain.

My doctor is a very funny guy. He also is very smart and experienced and has seen most everything. He began to tell me about his wife's brain surgery and his journey of faith. Then he rolled his stool over to my side of the room and grabbed me by the knees: "Well, Reverend Hull, it is time to believe." We talked about prayer and the spiritual side of the equation. I see science and faith as friends; where is the balance? Doctors are instruments. They can set a broken bone, but God heals the bones.

I left his office, got into my car, and began to cry. It was the first time I had been able to release the tension. People had been praying for me, and God had sent one of his chosen, my Jewish doctor who is on his own journey of faith. I was so embarrassed and ashamed for my lack of faith. I had to ask myself, *Why after all the prayer, Bible reading, retreats, seminars, years of writing books and helping people all over the world was I so weak?*

I told my home Bible study group this story and I cried and sobbed. I was able to get it all out only with assurances from my wife that I could do it. They seemed to understand it better than I did. My formation in Christ is like most others, except I am a licensed professional with theological degrees and have written a pile of books. I wanted to issue an immediate apology to all the people I have been impatient with when they couldn't believe God in some difficult situation. Like every other Christian, I am still in this process of becoming Christlike. I still am not sure what was going on and, yes, I eventually did get my hernia repaired. When I cried, when I confessed, I was finally able to say, *Okay, Lord, my days are in your hands. I can't control or add one day, one hour, one second more to my life through worry.*

I have spent more than forty years focused on being a disciple and making other disciples. You could say that people who know about such things might call me the discipleship man. So why should a weak man like me have such a task? Why should anyone listen to me? My only answer is that God has called me to it and the urge won't go away. It could be that my story in some way will help you in your struggle not to obey yourself. When I obey myself, I end up losing fifteen pounds because I can't eat; I have dark circles under my eyes; I spend hours in emergency rooms taking test after test. Then I talk about it endlessly to my wife and slip a sleeping pill under my tongue every night to get some rest. It sounds more like the kind of life Lucifer planned for me. He wants to steal my faith, kill my body, and destroy my joy. When you look in the mirror and see the light gone from your eyes, when you stop laughing or listening to music or thinking about a positive future, then Calvin's words: to obey yourself is life's great tragedy, penetrate, because you see a ruined man's reflection. But the words of Jesus restore my hope: "My purpose is to give them a rich and satisfying life" (John 10:10).

Reflections

The formation of Christ in a follower is a lifelong process. Life continues to amaze, challenge, and mostly surprise every person. One of the great surprises is how thin the veil between good and evil and that it remains thin all of our lives.

The crux of spiritual formation is that it is not primarily about becoming a better person but actually a different person. The process of spiritual formation is how the Holy Spirit acts on our inner person and changes us. This is made possible not from moral advancement based on science, reason, behaviorally based religion, or any other self-achievement narrative but by choosing to submit to Christ's leadership. This is commonly called discipleship.

But even when we undergo spiritual formation, the "flesh," that destructive part of the fallen nature, never improves. It continues to lurk just beneath the surface of even the most spiritually formed person. That is why our battle is not against "flesh and blood," as the apostle Paul so aptly put it (1 Corinthians 15:50, NIV).

Moreover, ease alone can cause us to lose ground that already had been gained through disciplined living. Medical professionals point out that hospital patients lose 50 percent of body strength in the first forty-eight hours of admittance due to inactivity. The point is, we never lose our need for spiritual growth, attention, intention, discipline, and being accountable in community. We don't reach a point where we can stop learning, trusting, and practicing the things that cause us to grow and develop into the image of Christ.

CHAPTER 4

A Disciple's Focus

Dietrich Bonhoeffer distilled the meaning of a disciple's life, saying, "It is nothing else than bondage to Jesus Christ alone, completely breaking through every programme, every ideal, every set of laws. No other significance is possible, since Jesus is the only significance. Beside Jesus nothing has any significance. He alone matters."[1]

One of the unique things about the Christian religion is its focus on becoming like its leader. God promises to actually inhabit each person who is born into a new life,[2] and this is what makes becoming like him possible. Islam does not exhort its followers to be like Mohammad. Buddhists are encouraged to learn from their leader, but Buddha did not claim to inhabit each of them. Mohammad and Buddha were normal men who reached extraordinary heights as humans and whom others came to admire. Jesus was different; he was, as G. K. Chesterton reportedly called him, "the everlasting man." In Christ, God became his own prophet and burst onto the scene, speaking with authority and performing miracles. He was so extraordinary that it took 451 years and ecumenical synods for the church to explain who he was.[3] No one really grasps it even now. "God in all his fullness was pleased to live in Christ" (Colossians 1:19). The only rational response is to bow before him and, like Thomas, declare, "My lord and my God!" (John 20:28).

Although the church fervently holds to the Trinity, there is no talk about becoming like the Father or the Holy Spirit. The Father commends and the Holy Spirit points to the Son. The goal of every believer is to be conformed to the image of Christ. Jesus puts a face on God; he demonstrates what God is like. Someone once said, "If God isn't like Jesus, he ought to be." The purpose of each of his followers is to become like Christ, as Paul wrote in Romans 8:28-30:

> We know that God causes everything to work together for the good of those who love God and are called according to his purpose for them. *For God knew his people in advance, and he chose them to become like his Son*, so that his Son would be the firstborn among many brothers and sisters. And having chosen them, he called them to come to him. And having called them, he gave them right standing with himself. And having given them right standing, he gave them his glory. (emphasis added)

C. S. Lewis observed that we are to become "little Christs." The church "exists for nothing else but to draw men into Christ, to make them little Christs. If they are not doing that, all the cathedrals, clergy, missions, sermons, even the Bible itself, are simply a waste of time. God became man for no other purpose."[4] Both Paul and Peter continued this theme.[5] We are told to follow in Christ's footsteps and to conform to his image.

In order to better understand what this means, let's spend some time examining conformity.

Why People Conform

When Paul told us not to be conformed to "this world," he was probably referring to the system of values, allurements, and "knowledge" that is hostile or indifferent toward God and his plans. He warned Christians not to allow the pressures of the world to conform them. This is an ever-present problem, and here the real battle is enjoined for the Christian.

The Enemy is far too crafty to think he can ruin many Christians with a frontal attack. He is much more interested in using the world system to create easy-to-mock caricatures of Christianity. He is delighted with people who believe they are standing strong for Christ when they march with placards declaring that God hates gays; it is here that the Devil knows he has destroyed their credibility. For years he has been able to convince good-hearted people that spirituality is keeping a set of strict rules and to separate themselves from the very people they are to love and reach. Even more interesting, he convinces others that being more hip and relevant is a way to reach the world. When this happens, churches become an echo chamber for what the world wants. The world says they want shorter services with less talk about sin, and churches serve it up, thinking it will help.

The allure of being accepted by people we admire possesses a powerful gravitational pull. This explains why people in the entertainment community are largely in agreement about politics and world events. They wear the same buttons and ribbons; they hold the same positions; they are a monolith with pizzazz. If you dare wander off the prescribed path, you are punished with less work in the community. This is human. If you respect an athlete, you are more inclined to adopt that person's viewpoint. Christians who come under the influence of intellectuals or a bohemian way of life tend to adapt their theology so they can gain the acceptance of those they admire. The warning here is, watch yourself carefully. Examine why you change views. Pay attention to who has influenced you and what it is you hope to gain by changing.

What causes people to conform? Youth are uniform in their non-conformity conformity. It is part of the search for identity for teens to reject their parent's conformity and develop their own form of conforming to one another. So we see boys wearing their pants so low that their boxer shorts become an important part of the outfit. Someone has convinced young women they should wear clothes that reveal both their strengths and weaknesses. Adults conform as well except in ways that cost us less. We face a daily reality that teens do not; it usually has to do with making a living. It comes down to what is the best deal. Life and even some research demonstrate that people conform when there is more to gain from conforming than from not conforming. This is no truer than when it comes down to being a follower of Christ. The reward for religious conformity is the acceptance by your faith community. When you gather together, there is edification, comfort, and encouragement.

Yet conforming to any religious group often involves sacrifices and some stigma.

Sacrifice and Stigma

Rodney Stark defines *stigma* as "all aspects of social deviance that is attached to membership in a religious group. Sacrifices consist of investments, material and human and forgone opportunities required of those who would gain and retain membership in the group."[6] The crucial issue for the church is this: What are the reasons for our stigmas and sacrifices, and are they the right reasons?

I grew up in a church that attached a lot of rules to the gospel, and conformity to those rules resulted in unnecessary stigma. Women wore long-sleeve dresses year round. They could not wear makeup or jewelry, and they did not cut their hair. This included not shaving the legs or under the arms. Church was the only place where I saw women like this until years later in Eastern Europe. There was something odd about seeing ten-year-old girls running and playing in long dresses on a hot summer day. There were unnecessary sacrifices as well. Members couldn't spend money on Sunday, play athletics on Sunday, dance, watch television, go to movies, or play any sport that required you to bare your legs. These rules were well-meaning, but they were based on some misguided interpretations of Scripture and a zeal for holiness. It has always been much easier to conform to a set of rules than to the example of Jesus.

It wasn't until years later that I learned that holiness, or *hagios*, simply means "set apart." The fact that God is holy means that he is separate; he is different. His attributes of love, patience, peacefulness, kindness, and so on are the qualities of holiness. Instead of saying holy, holy, holy, we might say different, different, different. Even so, when some people see a person who is dowdy or has chosen a life of poverty, they describe them as "holy." When the church gives someone a title, we assume that person is "godly." I think that is a mistake. It is so easy to get this wrong, to misname holiness, to pick out the wrong markers for it, and then to punish devout people with needless stigma and sacrifice.

What I'm saying is this: Let's make sure our conformity is to Christ, not to cultural Christianity. We are to be conformed to Christ, not to some aberrant form of a religious subculture. Let's be honest: The only reason there are different denominations is disagreement about Jesus or something he taught. Some will have a Republican Jesus who stands for a strong military, self-reliance, intelligent design, and all the other issues that go with that subculture. That, of course, is different than the Jesus who called us to preach to the poor, release the captives, and liberate people from the grip of the elite. This would be a green Jesus, who would be more politically left than right. Conforming to cultural Christianity is just another way we end up being conformed to the ways of the world. The Christian landscape is dotted with various camps of thought and traditions. People adopt the beliefs of a certain camp they join. Included in the beliefs are the cultural artifacts of each camp. Dressing, speaking, socializing, and voting the same way as your camp rewards you with affection, affirmation, and status.

In contrast to the stigmas and sacrifices that come with conformity to cultural Christianity, the early church experienced legitimate stigma and sacrifice. The primary stigma worth living or even dying for is the call upon every disciple's life to be a witness. The English word *witness* comes from the Greek word *martyr*, and of course this was and remains the most honored status for any Christian. The early Christians sacrificed by taking care of orphans, widows, and the unwanted. They also stayed and nursed people back to health during plagues. As stated earlier, the power of the gospel at work changed people's minds. It cost a lot to be a Christian in those days, but historically Christians have always considered this to be a good deal. Eternal life is the big payoff for a life of dedication and self-sacrifice in this present life.

One important observation about the early church is that stigma and sacrifice made for a more vibrant church and eliminated the majority of casual Christians. The removal of stigma and sacrifice from the Christian experience has increased the number of casual, or nominal, Christians. This deadwood steals much of a pastor's energy and time. Most pastors will tell you that the greatest suffering they have done for Christ has come at the hands of their own congregations. It seems to me that when Christians are committed to being faithful witnesses for Christ in their workplaces, neighborhoods, communities, and schools, they don't have time to beat up the pastor.

So what does it mean to be conformed to the image of Christ? First, let's clarify what it does *not* mean.

What Conforming to Christ Doesn't Look Like

Separatism

I was once acquainted with a man whose zeal to witness was legendary among his friends. If you were to meet him at a dinner party and he found out you were already a Christian, he would walk away from you. You no longer fit his target group. I was even worse. I used to exhibit an intense interest in my neighbors until they rejected my invitation to church. Then I lost interest in them. Both of these attitudes are a product of a separatist mindset. Separation from the world is a major conforming force in American churches today. I am convinced that churches that teach their people to treat the unbeliever as simply a "mark" will fail. They treat people as projects rather than objects of God's affection.

When you are conformed to the image of Christ, you value people for their intrinsic importance to God. Your assignment with a person is to love him or her as Christ loved, not to evaluate that individual's strategic importance to your mission. Separatism creates a "we-them" dichotomy that is dehumanizing to everyone.

Churches teach two kinds of separatism. One is physical, and those who practice it create a Christian alternative to every society the non-religious world has created. Much of it has been an effort to protect children from non-Christian children. All this money and effort has built a wall that is a hindrance to the spreading of the gospel. How different that is from the same church using money and effort to build mission hospitals and many other wonderful ministries to the needy. One insulates, and the other expands. To be "not of this world," as Jesus said, is good, but he never meant for us to be separate from the world. The entire idea of his kingdom narrative about wheat and weeds existing together makes the point that we must live among those who do not believe. To separate was never God's idea. He just told us not to marry unbelievers (see 2 Corinthians 6:14).

The second kind of separation that churches have taught is an emotional, or mental, one. It starts with a sense of superiority: "We have the truth, they don't, and they can't even know the truth because it is foolishness to them." This sense of superiority doesn't come from the same place as racism or entitlement. It is a slick kind of evil that finds its genesis in spiritual pride. It has a touch of pity in it that says, "Poor things. They are so lost, so blind! It's all so pathetic." When this is our attitude, we tell ourselves, *Unbelievers see the world differently. They don't value what I value, and I don't want my children to be influenced by them.* This becomes an excuse not to care or make an effort to befriend unbelievers. We don't mind preaching to them or debating with them, but to share life with them is close to unthinkable. The dogma of the church is to go to the world, but, in reality, our practice has been to separate. The irony is that we have separated ourselves, but we share the world's drive for success and for running our own lives.

The evil in this kind of conforming is that we are unprepared mentally, spiritually, and physically to reach unbelievers with the gospel. If you take the average church board member, you will find a person who has little personal contact with non-Christians. The classic problem of the church is that we spend so much time in church that we have no time to be the church. Yes, we do business with unbelievers, travel beside them, and live next door to them, but how many of us have caring relationships that yield invitations into their lives?

Conformity is not separation, nor is it moralism.

Moralism

Moralism is the belief that spirituality is about improving behavior and performance. It encourages the belief that I am worthwhile because I am a performing person. Many people would agree with the statement "The Christian's purpose is to be a better person, to be more moral, and to live according to higher standards." This moral performance narrative addresses guilt by trying harder. Dr. John Coe, in his very fine work in this area, defines the problem:

> Moral Temptation is the attempt of the hidden heart (not conscious) to try to perfect oneself in the power of the self, the attempt to use formation, the spiritual disciplines, good effort etc, to relieve the burden of spiritual failure, lack of love and the guilt and shame that results. To try and relieve that burden that Christ alone can relieve.[7]

Coe goes on to say that moralism is what we are saved from: a life of trying to be good and pleasing to God as a way to deal with our guilt and shame.[8]

Now, before you raise an eyebrow about the subconscious aspect to Coe's definition, let me explain. The use of the subconscious here is not to say in a Freudian way that we have no control over the lower regions of our nature. It is actually teaching a very Christian idea: that the "flesh" is programmed in its fallenness to automatically try to perform its way out of failure. Learning what God thinks about us and how he plans to improve us counteracts this. The short course is that God wills in us by his grace the ability to trust him and, therefore, to conform to his character. Yes, the growth process requires effort and discipline, but these are activated by the new life that is in us.

Moralism is most often experienced through the common exhortation to "straighten up and fly right." This addresses only the volition, or will, of the disciple; it appeals to shame and the idea that if we change, God's blessing and favor will return to us. This is slippery because God does appeal to our wills; he does ask us to repent. The primary difference between the moralist position and Scripture is that Scripture indicates that God is on our side and that we don't need to perform for his love and interest.[9] God is helping us work on our sin; we stand side by side with him, and we walk together.

Relevance is also on the list of things that conformity is not.

Relevance

The word *relevance* is the source of the word *relative*. For example, some say, "All truth is relative," by which they mean that there is no such thing as absolute truth. To be relevant means that someone or something becomes what it needs to be in order to meet a need. That need may change daily or hourly; cold medicine is relevant to a person with a cold but not to a healthy person. The desire to be relevant is normal and pays off in much of life. If you have the right product for sale at the right time, hula hoops or Hush Puppies, there is money to be made. If you start a church with an attractive ministry menu, people are likely to check it out.

The irony, however, is that relevance itself is relative. It rides the winds of change, and if you consider it the key to success, you will find yourself swept away on its whim. The only reliable relevance is finding out how one's life can be relevant to God, and that does not change. The only true relevance is rooted in the eternal. There are certain fixed truths about the human experience; they have been established from eternity past. These truths are the unmovable ground on which we stand.

Our concern here is to expose the foolishness of being relevant as a conforming influence to the shaping of human personality. The most common expression is the desire to be accepted by peers, business associates, and, of course, the opposite sex. This influences the clothes we wear, the cars we drive, the language we use, the food we eat, the movies we see, the music we listen to, and the books we read. At a certain level, this is normal, healthy, and necessary to society. However, the danger of being driven by relevance is that personhood is threatened; a person's identity is shaped by unmet needs for acceptance and recognition. The problem is that you become a product of an ever-changing environment. You have no place to stand, no moral or spiritual home. The religious life lends itself to forming people who want to be hip in order to build a ministry; therefore, the only thing that nourishes the soul is the spiritual fast food of results.

Jesus was irrelevant to Israel's political and spiritual expectations. Even his own followers expected some sort of political or military rescue from the Romans. Jesus wasn't a zealot seeking political power, or a Pharisee trying to cleanse the nation of sinful practices. He was a man of downward mobility, of humble service to others. He was also the most relevant person who ever lived. His relevancy came from his person, from his non-changing character, from his unwillingness to conform to the powerful forces of his religious culture.

Now let's examine what conformity to Christ *does* look like.

What Conformity to Christ Looks Like

There are a number of ways to discuss what conformity to Christ looks like. One method would be to comb the gospels and point out from the narration the traits and qualities Jesus displayed. Another would be to note how Jesus lived out the Beatitudes or the fruit of the Spirit. Both approaches would be appropriate, but I prefer to use Paul's summary of Jesus' character in Philippians 2:5-8:

You must have the same attitude that Christ Jesus had.

Though he was God,
   he did not think of equality with God
   as something to cling to.
Instead, he gave up his divine privileges;
   he took the humble position of a slave
   and was born as a human being.
When he appeared in human form,
   he humbled himself in obedience to God
   and died a criminal's death on a cross.

According to this passage, we are conforming to Christ when our lives demonstrate humility, submission, obedience, and sacrifice.

Humility

Winston Churchill was famous for saying about a political opponent that he was as a humble man because he had much to be humble about. Humility comes to a person who grasps that all gifts, talents, opportunities, and accomplishments are from the hand of God. It is rare to hear a person take credit for all his or her accomplishments; even the most secular award recipients give God and others some credit.

Humility is the starting line for putting on Christ; its absence makes conforming to Christ impossible. God stands in opposition to any person who doesn't have it.[10] Humility attracts God's grace, and just as surely, pride runs it off. I would define humility as the acknowledgement of who or what you are dependent on. Humility's power is that it frees a person to focus on others; it opens the door to begin to affect others as Christ did.

Jesus' attitude was one of humility, which comes from the Latin *humus*, which means earth or dirt. Philippians 2 testifies that Jesus took a humble position in that he became a human being. Because of his humility, Jesus was able to fit into the larger purpose of redemption. He did not cling to what so many of us think we need: recognition and the right to be treated with respect. Jesus was God, but he didn't insist on being treated as such. He lost his status as God, suffered at the hands of the people he came to help, and even felt abandoned by his Father.

It often takes a person who has endured tough times to communicate humility with power. People who have lost their health, money, or the limelight tell the most moving stories. When we lose our pride, lay aside our desire to control, decide to obey and live for others, humility becomes our habit. It makes its way into our character through the regular practice of prayer, through the assimilation of God's Word, and in living for others.

Submission

Submission is motivated by love; any other force that can yield submission is limited. Forced submission does not feed the soul, nourish the spirit, or bring joy to one's life, which is why people who are freed from oppressive relationships in their families or businesses or even from criminal prosecution no longer submit to their oppressors. Jesus, however, modeled a submission that was fueled by love; therefore, it endured and had no limits. He submitted to his Father's will, which was for him to give up the privileges of divinity. There was no limit to Jesus' willingness to serve the Father he loved. The more he submitted to God's will, the more joy it brought him because he was pleasing the one he loved. That is the model of all human relationships, which is something we will consider later. For now, however, let it be said that submission is the fruit of humility. The two together form the identity of Jesus. When his disciples follow his example and submit to the Father out of love, their lives have a transformative effect on those they come in contact with. When a person submits and serves from a basis of love, that person is free from self-interest, and the joy comes through.

This truth is beautifully illustrated in the film *Babette's Feast*, which is based on a story by Isak Dinesen. It begins with a portrait of two spinsters, Martine and Phillipa, whose father is the leader of a strict religious sect. The sisters are tempted to leave the village and live the "life of sin," but in the end, both women settle down to assist their father. Over time the father dies and the sect doesn't produce joy, love, and acceptance. In fact, most of the relationships in the village are broken or damaged by slights, gossip, and misunderstandings. Babette is a former great chef in Paris who has moved to the sister's village. When she miraculously wins the lottery, she offers to prepare a meal for the sisters in honor of their father. People gather for the feast. When the guests sit down and begin to eat, they are impressed with the sauces. The taste of the food creates words of praise, indeed a sensual pleasure. The experience has power that melts the guest's defenses. As they enjoy the feast, their attitudes begin to soften and people begin to apologize. In one of the most poignant scenes, two women who have not spoken to each other for many years touch foreheads affectionately, saying, "God bless you." One woman begins to sing, and a man rises and quotes Psalm 85:10: "Unfailing love and truth have met together. Righteousness and peace have kissed." The story illustrates the healing of relationships, a rebirth of community. Babette loved people for their own sake. She used what she had: a little money and skill. Her act of love, based in humility, changed lives.

Obedience

Jesus' humble act of submission led to the only thing that mattered: obedience. Dietrich Bonhoeffer put it well when he said, "Faith is only real in obedience."[11] Christian spirituality finds its only meaning in obedience. Any other destination for what we call our spiritual worldview would discredit it. The only road to a life of satisfying obedience is one paved with humility and submission. When the word *obedience* stands alone, it feels austere, possibly even legalistic. Jesus never thought of obedience as a sterile act of courage; it was his heart responding to his Father, another way of saying, "I love you." For him, obedience to the Father was uncomplicated and heartfelt.

Sacrifice

Sacrifice is the natural result of humility, submission, and obedience. Jesus' sacrifice was the greatest and most outrageous in the history of humanity. Not only did he choose the indignity of taking on a body, even in this very hour he continues to inhabit such a limited container; he continues to bear the wounds of his execution.

What might sacrifice look like in Christ's followers today? Contemporary sacrifice in the West is a bit nuanced. In America and Western Europe, one can still speak their religious mind without fear of jail. I believe this will change in the next decade; it will become illegal to speak of the falsehood of other religions under the guise of hate speech. Most Christians in the West should be more concerned about the serious decline in evangelical faith. It is wobbling seriously at this time and if things remain the same will soon fall on its face onto the hard ground of relativism. When evangelicals give up on hell and the exclusiveness of Christ, Christianity will no longer be a threat to the Enemy or a serious solution to evil. The sacrifice of today's disciple will be taking a stand and being labeled for it, being hated for it, and losing friends over it.

Every martyr or person who suffers for the cause of Christ is his colleague, yet Christ's sacrifice stands above all others because of who he is and where he came from. Although he was perfect, he was executed as a criminal. Because no one born in sin can be innocent in the way Jesus came to us, his death was the greatest injustice in history. As those who knew him claimed, "He never sinned, nor ever deceived anyone" (1 Peter 2:22). Paul chimed in for the ages, "He made him who knew no sin to be sin on our behalf, so that we might become the righteousness of God in Him" (2 Corinthians 5:21, NASB). Jesus bore our sins, bearing the cost of them. Now we are free to do the same for others. That is where our sacrifice comes from. I love the words of John Stott: "The essence of sin is we human beings substituting ourselves for God, while the essence of salvation is God substituting himself for us."[12] All of life's opportunities to sacrifice are where we substitute ourselves in someone else's place to serve.

Jesus was a man for others, as Bonhoeffer called him. That is his essence. He needed no one, but he chose to serve others, to build his life around other lives. This is why the simple reality that "God so loved the world that he gave his one and only Son, that whoever believes in him shall not perish but have eternal life" (John 3:16, NIV) burst into the Greco-Roman world and changed it. Jesus is someone to worship who is not capricious; he won't trick you, take advantage of you, or break promises. He is a person you can count on, who has already given himself fully for you. He is the difference between being loved and living in an impersonal universe where you are no more special than a blob of primordial slime. The goal of disciples is to take on his character.

Reflections

Conforming is not the challenge. Just walk through a shopping mall, attend a rock concert, or watch a television program and you'll see people wearing the same style clothes, using the same phrases, catch words, and profanity. Everyone can and does conform. The challenge is conforming in a way that makes you a "little Christ"—someone who thinks, acts, and feels like Jesus about others and the world. In order to do this, you must know what to avoid and you must know what to pursue.

People, events, and institutions are powerful forces that shape us, and it is difficult not to conform to them and their values. To the degree that they follow Christ, then good, but there is always the need for discernment. This is especially true in church, because that is where we are the most vulnerable. In church our defenses are at their lowest and our desire to please is at its height. In order to conform to religious society, we must take on some stigma and make sacrifices. For example, as Christ followers, we might take on the stigma of being narrow-minded and will be asked to make sacrifices, such as giving away 10 percent of our income. What is to be avoided is often what many find the most attractive: living separate from the unbeliever, dedicating ourselves to moral behavior through legalism or strict rules, and being relevant to the unbeliever through compromise or diluting the Christian message.

Instead, make it your focus to better understand how Jesus would live your life, in your set of circumstances. This is much more profound than asking, "What would Jesus do?" in a particular situation. This is to understand who Jesus is so that you can know what he might do. Ask yourself, *What are his character traits? How can I display these traits in my job? In my home? In my neighborhood?* Focus on the four characteristics of Jesus: humility, submission, obedience, and sacrifice. These qualities — when practiced in community, Christian and non-Christian alike — are revolutionary.

CHAPTER 5

Real Change Always "Shows Up"

Which comes first, the chicken or the egg? Is character transformation more being than doing, more internal than external? Actors address this issue when they practice their craft. Sometimes they begin on the inside, with how the script describes the character, and create an internal, emotional structure that is the basis for that character's speech and actions. Other times they start on the outside, with the character's clothes, voice, and facial expressions. For example, in the film *Rainman*, actor Dustin Hoffman worked inside out, while in *Tootsie*, where he dressed and portrayed a woman, he worked outside in.

It's much the same with followers of Jesus. God works both inside out and outside in. Transformation—real and lasting change—finds its roots on the inside of a person but will always "show up" in different behavior that affects others. For that reason, it is impossible to become like Christ in the passive voice. Waiting for something to happen to you is hope unattached to truth. While we can't explain the mystery of the human will and God's action, we do know that the Bible is written to someone who is an active participant in "putting off the old and taking on the new." Colossians 3 and Ephesians 4 both talk about the process.

The Classic View of Spiritual Formation

There is a difference of opinion on how people change. The classic position is that people change on the inside and that change works itself out into the social world. Solomon mentions a very ordinary manifestation of the relationship between internal and external: "A glad heart makes a happy face; a broken heart crushes the spirit" (Proverbs 15:13).

Dallas Willard, who is a proponent of this view, writes,

> Let me say to you very formally: Christian spiritual forma-
> tion is the process through which the embodied/reflective will
> takes on the character of Christ's will. It is the process through
> which (and you know Gal. 4:19) Christ is formed in you and
> me. Think of Paul's magnificent statement: "The life which I
> live in the flesh I live by the faith of the Son of God who loved
> me and gave himself for me." Not faith in, but the faith of.
> I have taken his faith into me. *I am now being inwardly the
> person that Christ has called me to be, and this inward faith has
> now spread throughout my socially embodied self.*[1]

Spiritual formation begins inside with the choice to act on the power of Christ that resides in us. In Romans 6–8, Colossians 2–3, and Galatians 2–3 and 5, Paul addressed the status of a Christian as a spiritually adopted child who struggles with a dual nature. He instructed that the receptive parts of us choose to act in the power of Christ. On a more theological level, he explained the psycho/spiritual-somatic nature of human personality and how it can be transformed into being our servant rather than our being its slave. Spiritual formation has to do with spirituality (internal) and habit (external).

In *The Screwtape Letters*, C. S. Lewis puts it well. Uncle Screwtape scolds the apprentice demon Wormwood for permitting his patient to become a Christian. "There is no need to despair; hundreds of these adult converts have been reclaimed after a brief sojourn in the enemy's camp and are now with us. All habits of the patient, both mental and bodily, are still in our favor."[2] The issue is spirituality and habit; the disciple is responsible to take effective action by engaging in habits that will be transformational and will enable him or her to take on the character of Christ.

Scripture is addressed to Christians with built-in receptors planted by God and the Holy Spirit at spiritual birth. There is an expectation that we will act. As Willard points out,

> One of the ironies of spiritual formation is that every "spiritual" discipline is a bodily behavior. We have to involve the body in spiritual formation because that's where we live and what we live from. So now spiritual formation is formation of the inner being of the human being, resulting in transformation of the whole person, including the body in its social context. *Spiritual formation is never merely inward.*[3]

God works inside out through prayer, Bible reading, and the practice of spiritual exercises, yet these actions require the cooperation of the body, and external elements are vital. Jesus told those who liked to pray for public display to find a prayer closet. Putting the body in a place of solitude is both an internal decision and an external action. The decision to serve others requires us to transport ourselves to another location, which is what we call "showing up." For the disciple, being is not more important than doing. Both are required for spiritual formation, for lasting change.

We've seen that the internal does affect the external, but can the external change the internal?

Can Actions Contrary to Natural Desire Change Us?

Some Christians have overreacted to legalism, or moralism, and so discount the role of outward behavior to real change. These folks have a naïve enchantment with the spiritual life through sacred place and withdrawal. Those whose trust is in contemplation are as wrong as those who trust skill development as a means to spiritual strength.

The question remains, *Does action that is against one's natural desire create a new or different spirit in a person?* To answer this, I need to ask a question that is rarely asked: "To whom is God talking when he exhorts us to believe, serve, or obey? More specifically, when he exhorts us to "count yourselves dead to sin but alive to God in Christ Jesus" (Romans 6:11, NIV) and "get rid of all bitterness, rage, anger, harsh words, and slander" (Ephesians 4:31)? There are hundreds of more commands like these. To whom is God talking?

I suppose most people figure, *He's talking to me*, and resist the temptation to dissect the question. Others consider the question crucial to a person's spiritual formation. Some would rather leave it a mystery and say that God is addressing all humans. But I disagree. Christians are given a special interest and capacity to obey because God inhabits us (see Colossians 1:27; 2:9; John 15:5-13). I hesitate to enter this theological quagmire, but hang with me and I think we will survive the journey.

Christians have two sides to the immaterial person. There is the "I" that wants to please God and says, "I love God's law with all my heart" (Romans 7:22). There is also the "flesh," which Paul called "another power within me that is at war with my mind" (verse 23). Paul put it much like we would. His mind had decided to trust God, but another force deep inside him — the "flesh" — pushed him to trust himself and maintain control. Here's another way Paul described this struggle: "I have been crucified with Christ; it is no longer I who live, but Christ who lives in me; and the life I now live in the flesh I live by faith in the Son of God, who loved me and gave himself for me" (Galatians 2:20, RSV).

Note that Paul used the word *flesh* differently here to mean a human body. It was not his mind and body alone that lived, but Christ also lived in him and enabled him to choose Christ's way. Every day he faced a battle between these two sides. He knew what he should and wanted to do, but he sometimes failed. It's the same with us. Perhaps this is why Jesus told all of us who would follow him to take up our cross daily. We have made a decision to be his disciple, but every day there are smaller decisions that either confirm or deny that larger decision.

Here's an example of what this might look like. Let's say you have a strong dislike for some work associates. It is just that you don't like them. Perhaps they have a tic or an irritating laugh or they always butt in when you are talking. As a disciple of Christ, you know you are to love even your enemies. You are dreading that you are about to be stuck with them in a car for four hours on an important business trip. How will you treat them? Would you consider asking God to give you a couple of ideas for how you might bless them, help them in some way, or even give them gifts? If your response is, "No way—I can't even ponder such nonsense," I would suggest you are spiritually dull or deadened.

I would further suggest that the way to create new vitality in your spirit is to dedicate yourself to loving your work associates until they "get it" that you love them. Isn't this what Jesus meant when he taught us, "You have heard the law that says, 'Love your neighbor' and hate your enemy. But I say, love your enemies! Pray for those who persecute you! In that way, you will be acting as true children of your Father in heaven" (Matthew 5:43-45)? We are to act as a "true child" of God, even when we don't feel like acting.

Abraham Heschel speaks frankly to this issue:

> The world needs more than the secret holiness of individual inwardness. It needs more than sacred sentiments and good intentions. Man's power of action is less vague than his power of intention. And as action of intrinsic meaning, its value to the world is independent of what it means to the person performing it. The act of giving food to a helpless child is meaningful regardless of whether or not the moral intention is present. God asks for the heart, and we must spell our answer in terms of deeds.[4]

When a convicted felon serving a sentence of community service hands a bowl of soup to a hungry person, there is value in that action, regardless of the server's motivation. And I would go further. Compulsory kindness creates something positive in the server's inner life; it changes them. The judge who sentenced the felon to feed the hungry represents a society that believes this is a good assignment for the lawbreaker. There is a natural law of conscience that innately knows that a good action taken by a person under compulsion can change the nature of that person. Karl Barth wrote, "Since conscience is the perfect interpreter of life, what it tells us is no question, no riddle, no problem, but a fact—the deepest, innermost, surest fact of life: God is righteous."[5] When a person acts like God would act, it shapes that person's attitude.

Of course, we must be careful how we seek to help others. Matthew warns,

> Watch out! Don't do your good deeds publicly, to be admired by others, for you will lose the reward from your Father in heaven. When you give to someone in need, don't do as the hypocrites do—blowing trumpets in the synagogues and streets to call attention to their acts of charity! I tell you the truth, they have received all the reward they will ever get. But when you give to someone in need, don't let your left hand know what your right hand is doing. Give your gifts in private, and your Father, who sees everything, will reward you. (Matthew 6:1-4)

When the intention of the action is to serve others as a "little Christ," there is a reward for that action. What might that reward be? I think it would be a mistake to push it all into the afterlife, to jewels, medals, or other good stuff in the heavenly realm. I think the reward is a transformed spirit, which begins in the here and now and lasts for eternity. Jesus said the reason he taught his disciples to love and obey him was that their joy would be made full (see John 15:11). If we repeatedly act kind, even when we are not feeling kind, we begin to be kind. The external will change the internal.

Some might point out that a few people, such as Hitler, Stalin, and Mao, are so cynical that they can pass out flowers to some schoolchildren while killing other schoolchildren at another location. But we are talking about the process of spiritual transformation in a disciple of Christ. God rewards kind acts in his children through the law of repeated action, which creates habits that then become our character.

Reflections

Real and lasting change finds its root on the inside of a person and always "shows up" in different behavior that affects others. The mystery of human will and God's action remains a mystery, but we do know that the Bible is written to someone who is to act, and that someone is the disciple quickened to life through spiritual birth. The new person within responds to the commands of Christ. The new person is not passive but an active participant in his or her own salvation and in putting off the old and replacing it with the new.

Action is less vague than intention; it begins with intention but is unknown to others without the act. For example, I intended on a whim to pick up my grandson the other day and take him out to breakfast. However, I didn't do it because of other events. My grandson never knew that I intended to pick him up and neither did anyone else.

Inner change is not easily distinguished from external change, but to the extent that it is, I would rate it the first in the chain of action. People change and then affect others. Therefore, changed people create networks or groups that are a reflection of that change. It should be noted that a network formed from internally changed people creates a powerful force for change and influences culture. This is why the church is essential: an army of changed people will do more than just a few. This is obvious but largely ignored. The church so often begins with the external — the network, the action — and wonders why energy fades. It fades because it was not firmly placed in the inner person.

CHAPTER 6

The Only Path to Spiritual Transformation

The Word of God is to be eaten, taken into our bodies like food. We consume it, and it digests in us and affects our minds, spirits, and bodies. That's why Jewish rabbis put honey on the fingers of their young male students and have them smear it on a tablet. The boys are then instructed to lick the tablet to taste the sweetness of the Torah, the Law of God. Taking in the Word of God is to be a total sensory experience because it is to change everything about us, head to toe.

The only way any of us can experience life is through the body, the only way others can experience us is through our bodies, and the only way we can experience new life in Christ is through the body. One can't divorce inner change from outer change. When the Scriptures command me to act, I cannot take the action without the cooperation of my body. Think about it: When I am speaking to a group, they see my body; they don't see my spirit. For this reason, the spiritual disciplines are focused on the body. Silence, solitude, fasting, frugality, chastity, sacrifice, study, prayer—all call upon the body to submit. Actions are less vague than words, and words are less vague than thoughts. When people experience me, it is as a six-foot-six, 225-pound, white-haired man. The sound of my voice, the various expressions on my face, and the movement of my arms work together to make an impression. If my body had been harmed by a serious accident or disease, the impression I make on others would be different. My appearance could foster compassion if I were restricted to a wheelchair or create questions if I were

morbidly obese. Regardless, somehow my spirit gets out and through my body to others. And that determines how people view me. That's why a person with an ugly or deformed body can seem beautiful to others and a magnificent physical specimen can be repulsive. The following quote, which describes the great literary genius Samuel Johnson and how people responded to him, illustrates this point:

> A nasty old man, a giant in both body and mind, always absent-minded, fierce, touchy, dirty, full of unpleasant habits, always shifting his body when he is seated, and always moving his jaw like an ox chewing the cud; but as he is rightly believed to possess more learning than any other man in this kingdom, he is feared and respected by all, perhaps more than he is loved.[1]

Johnson's body, even while repulsive to some, was transformed to the point that Christ came through and caused his friends to love him, even to find him endearing.

I want to drive home the point that taking in the Word of God is a total experience for the whole person. The Bible says that transformation begins in the mind (see Romans 12:2). But that is preceded by the command to put your body on the altar as a living sacrifice. You just can't do this without the body; the whole corpus needs to be transformed. The posture of the body, the look in the eyes, the tone of voice, our facial expressions — it all matters. It is all a product of assimilation of the Word of God.

My wife is an artist, a very good one I might add. She is always working on some kind of project, be it writing, painting, sculpture, or design. One summer she created some free-spirited paintings that she left hanging on a makeshift gallery, the backyard fence. I enjoyed them in our garden and commented on how much they added to our summer evenings. We had been debating for some time about what kind of art we wanted above the dining room table. She didn't like what we had there. I did. I liked it very much. Then one day, I walked into the dining room and saw that she had replaced the painting I liked with one from her garden gallery. In that moment, it became apparent by my facial expression, my tone of voice, and my general demeanor that I was not allowing the Word of God to transform my reaction. "Ugh," I grunted. "That doesn't look right. It's okay for the garden but not here. It doesn't meet the standard." Jane didn't say much, but a few minutes later, I heard something like kicking, stomping, and things breaking. I walked into the kitchen and found her stomping her painting, ripping the canvas, breaking the wood, and then cramming it into the trash bin. There was silence, one of shock and awe. It lasted for a few hours. I thought, *Oops.* My wife had experienced me, my body. Through my body, I had communicated in so many ways without saying much at all. The Word of God must be taken in. Its role is to transform us in all the ways others experience us.

The Word of God does not fluctuate like our emotions, nor will we mistake an inner voice for God's voice in our humanness. When we place the Holy Scriptures first, then other forms of godly communication can come to us as auxiliary, which they always are.

Putting on the Mind of Christ

Transformation begins in that part of the immaterial nature called the mind. That's why Paul told us, "Do not be conformed to this world *but be transformed by the renewal of your mind*, that you may prove what is the will of God, what is good and acceptable and perfect" (Romans 12:2, rsv, emphasis added). The first part of the exhortation puts the priority on change, and it locates the starting point as the mind. The second part speaks to the affect of a changed person on those around him or her. God places in each believer a visceral hunger for him, along with a desire to please him.

Why would a person want to change his or her mind, to put on "the mind of Christ" (1 Corinthians 2:16)? When a person is regenerated, all things have become new (see 2 Corinthians 5:17), including the desire to please God and to prove his perfect will. According to Philippians 2:12-13, the Holy Spirit causes the human spirit to desire to submit to God's will: "As you have always obeyed, so now, not only as in my presence but much more in my absence, work out your own salvation with fear and trembling; for *God is at work in you*, both *to will* and *to work* for his good pleasure" (RSV, emphasis added).

Christian spiritual formation is distinctive from other forms of spiritual formation because it begins and ends with Christ. When a person is in Christ, that individual possesses the desire and the capacity to change. God is at work in you, and he gives the disciple the will to submit to a pattern of life that leads to character transformation. God is willing us to act in ways that agree with his good pleasure; he is willing us to perform acts that please him. This is the beauty of submitting to God's direction. He wills certain desires in us that we can then act on. This process frees us from trying to do and accomplish everything that should be done. We participate in the part of his kingdom only in the way that he has planned for us. We do the work that he wants us to do.

Dallas Willard makes an important distinction between discipleship and spiritual formation that can help clarify how this works. He states that discipleship is the decision to follow Jesus, to be his apprentice. This is about positioning yourself, making yourself available for God to use you. Spiritual formation, on the other hand, is the direct action of the Holy Spirit upon the inner person.[2]

Transformation begins when we act.

Put Your Nose in Scripture

Second Timothy 3:16-17 tells us, "All scripture is inspired by God and profitable for teaching, for reproof, for correction, and for training in righteousness, that the man of God may be complete, equipped for every good work" (RSV). Scripture has always been the primary source for knowing God's identity, what kind of being he is, and the nature of his plan for the world, us, and eternity. God gave humankind spoken language to communicate his thoughts to us. At one time, he communicated with us only through oral tradition. Eventually, this oral tradition became the written document that we know as the Old Testament. In Paul's words to Timothy, the young pastor was reading a letter that neither he nor Paul knew would be included in Holy Writ. The New Testament was a growing portfolio of letters and histories with the mission to explain what happened with Jesus and to correct excesses and mistakes of those who were then following him. So when Paul said "Word of God," he was referring to that body of written truth that at that time was recognized by the believing community as from God. By 397 AD, that believing community had decided that the twenty-seven books of the New Testament were authoritative and part of God's written Word.[3]

Whatever the Word of God was then, we know what it is now, and it is the basis for completeness of a disciple.[4] That completeness is more than skill; it involves a process that includes being taught, reproved, corrected, and trained.[5] This process of transformation is from the Spirit. It can be painful and frustrating, and it starts with God's Word acting on our minds. Scripture tells us what is right. When we go astray, it shows us that it is wrong. It puts us back on the right path and then encourages us to train, to make the new ideas that have renewed our minds our habit and therefore our character. The Word of God is necessary to our spiritual formation because it uses the vehicle of language to make God's thoughts our thoughts. Because we have the Word of God, we can believe what Jesus believed. We can see the world the way he saw it, and we can even feel about it the way he felt about it.

The Word of God also does something in our spiritual formation that even the most clever psychologist or spiritual guru cannot accomplish. God uses his Word to reveal things about ourselves that are secret to us. Scripture can reveal to us our motivations, both selfish and spiritual. As the following passage says, "Before him no creature is hidden, but all are open and laid bare to the eyes of him with whom we have to do" (Hebrews 4:13, rsv).

When we read the Scriptures with our hearts open to the Holy Spirit, nothing is hidden. God lays us open; his eyes see perfectly into our inner person. When we submit to the message of his Word, we are not just engaging in a religious rite; we are engaged in an intimate dialogue with God himself. Hebrews 4:12 speaks of the precise nature of God's words: "The word of God is living and active, sharper than any two-edged sword, piercing to the division of soul and spirit, of joints and marrow, and discerning the thoughts and intentions of the heart" (rsv).

No Other Path

There is no other path to Christian spiritual transformation than through meaningful interaction with the Word of God. Many Christians have tried to change without its penetrating analysis, but they have failed. The nature of Scripture is to address the internal first, but it does not detach thought from behavior. It does not allow us to sit alone on a high place, separated from life, simply pondering doing what is right. It does not permit us to continue to lie or steal while our immaterial nature ponders a change in behavior. It assumes a direct and immediate link between thought and action.

True thoughts find their rightful home in the Scriptures, and they find their way into the disciple's mind through reading and prayerful reflection. But it is also true that those same truths come to mind through the spoken words of others, and even events. God sometimes reminds the disciple that something contained in the Word of God is immediately relevant to the moment. In a Christian community, the truth of God's Word is in members whose minds it has transformed. So both internal scriptural reflection and external exhortation and life experience contribute to our transformation.

And, as was pointed out in the previous chapter, don't sell short the power of doing the right thing, even when our heart is not quite in it. For it is especially in those moments that we make some of our greatest strides toward Christlikeness. In fact, the immediate right action is the best tonic for creating a strengthened motivation in a person. For example, God asked Cain concerning his depressed emotional state, "Why are you so angry? . . . Why do you look so dejected? You will be accepted if you do what is right. But if you refuse to do what is right, then watch out! Sin is crouching at the door, eager to control you. But you must subdue it and be its master" (Genesis 4:6-7). These questions went to the heart of Cain's character: *What pleased him or did not please him? What was he willing or not willing to do?* God was, to use a contemporary phrase, telling Cain that he needed to be reprogrammed, that he was of a certain character, and that a new one could be formed. Cain could be reformed, transformed, changed if he did what was right. He could become the kind of person who would desire to do right and would experience pleasure when he did. In Cain's case, God's words were spoken. For us, almost always, they are written. The Word of God becomes our counselor, for it alone, with the help of the Holy Spirit, can discern with precision what changes are to be made in us.

Resist Trying to Thread the Needle

It is tempting to contemplate what actually triggers personality change in us. By personality, I am referring to the transformation of a person to the degree that others notice the change. We might ask ourselves, *Are my motives pure? Why exactly am I doing this?* I don't think we can know that, nor can we peel one layer of motivation from another with any accuracy. The practice of the truth is much more transformational than the mere knowledge of the truth. Giving five dollars to a homeless person is less vague and more useful than whispering a prayer for the homeless.

All action regardless of motivation is good if it is in submission to the truth of Scripture. I distinguish here that "the truth of Scripture" means a proper interpretation and application of the same. Many people have misinterpreted Scripture and then misapplied it to everyone's harm, among the most notable being misapplication of Scripture to justify slavery and the atrocities done during the Crusades. This is still being done today. Some Christians say that God told them to divorce their mate or take vengeance on a neighbor.

There is a mystery of the human will and God's sovereignty. This always has been and always will be. We know there is a struggle; we know we have made good choices and bad choices. But when we try to figure out if a bad decision was God's decision because it was part of his larger sovereign plan, we create more problems and no answers. What's important to remember is that God uses both internal and external stimulus to change us into the image of his Son. He does this through so many things. For example, we can read a passage of Scripture the Holy Spirit embeds in our soul; it therefore creates action in us. Or a person may speak a word to us that breaks through some barriers. In my own case, friends have given me gifts of time, counsel, money, goods, and services, and these gifts have contributed to my reshaping into the image of Christ. My memory comes alive when I recall a close friend slipping a five-dollar bill into my hand when my wife and I had nothing for groceries. God has also used negative external experiences to shape me: the travails of travel, the opposition of enemies, the betrayal of friends, and the slackness of the nominal Christians.

So don't punish yourself with excessive introspection. It has been said, "The unexamined life is not worth living." I would not disagree, but I would recommend leaving that part to someone equipped for the job: God himself.

> Search me, O God, and know my heart;
>> test me and know my anxious thoughts.
> Point out anything in me that offends you,
>> and lead me along the path of everlasting life.
>> (Psalm 139:23-24)

If I try to obey the Bible's exhortation to "put off the old person and put on the new," who is choosing to do that? Me or the new person in me? Is there a difference? Being the fool I am, I would suggest that God is appealing to the new person within, which is God himself, who has taken up residence in me. Once a person is "in Christ," God is at work to will and to work all things. When our urges and desires match God's Word and leading, we should act on them. We should expect to make some mistakes. This is normal and accepted. But being paralyzed by the fear of failure is not.

Reflections

Spiritual formation begins within. Its primary tool is to take a God-given desire to change and reform a person's mind with God's thoughts. A renewed mind, fueled by a Holy Spirit–birthed desire, creates new actions, which become habits, and habits are what make our character.

CHAPTER 7

Being with God

The first time I read Revelation 3:20, "Behold, I stand at the door, and knock: if any man hear my voice, and open the door, I will come in to him" (KJV), was in the booklet *The Four Spiritual Laws*. The context was inviting Christ into my life as a first act of faith that would "save me." I took it to mean that Jesus would come into my life, but the verse didn't give me any detail about what he wanted to do once I opened the door. I went on my way as a Christ follower and viewed this invitation as the first step in the Christian experience. Like a number of things Christian, my relationship with God became a utilitarian functional fact. I went through a long season of searching for a more personal, alive faith — one that would make my blood run hot and move my emotions. I wanted a faith that would thaw my frozen soul. So when I came across the same verse in the New Living Translation — "Look! I stand at the door and knock. If you hear my voice and open the door, I will come in, and we will share a meal together as friends" — I read it with new eyes. I realized that Jesus actually wants to spend time with me.

I had been teaching for many years that God wants to have a personal relationship with everyone, but I believed that my relationship with him revolved around the mission he assigned me. I also knew that the "personal relationship" term had been used by fundamentalists in the early part of the twentieth century to combat a more impersonal liberal gospel being proposed by the modernists. It meant to me that

I was to check in with God about how I was doing and also get further instructions. So I talked to him in prayer about my needs and my family and friends, but it almost always centered around my being able to accomplish the mission. I assumed that my family and my personal emotions and desires were a means to an end. That end, of course, was my religious duty to make disciples. My family was secondary to that mission. My attitude was, *God, if I put you and your work first, then I expect you to take care of my family.*

I had heard this from many a "man of God." But time is a powerful tutor, and it has taught me about the impact of one family. It has shown me that I was naïve about the power of a family. I was the selfish one who thought my family was there for me to do God's work when, in fact, they have been at the center of my work. They also have played the major role in my being spiritually formed. Relating to the same people for forty years is a necessary school for the development of Christian human personality. My family's role in my life during the fun, joy, heartache, and conflict has shaped me more than any other experience. My fellowship with the members of my family has greatly influenced my fellowship with God. I have come to believe that the real power of a person is in his or her private or common life. How much one of my books impacts a pastor somewhere in Australia is important to the kingdom of God, but the book doesn't influence him as much as his wife, his children, and those with whom he lives in community do. I don't expect my readers to surround me and hold my hand as I die; it will be my family and friends. My sons and their wives and children will remember me long after my readers have discarded my work. My children are more likely to be permanent carriers of my beliefs and legacy. I now believe that my family is my most important contribution; they have made my public life possible. I will leave behind more than twenty books, hundreds of articles, many DVDs, and two sons. I'll put my money on my sons, and their sons, and their sons. (Daughters are great, but there aren't any yet!)

Up until the day I read Revelation 3:20 with new eyes, I hadn't thought much about what discipleship might look like beyond personal salvation. I had plenty of ideas, programs, and books and had heard a lot of sermons on the life of a disciple, but I had missed that God wants to get to know me as friend. When I meet a friend for lunch, we catch up on family, health, and friends. We talk about how things are going in each of our lives. Although this may seem basic to some, I find it profound that God wants this kind of friendship with me.

What Kind of Relationship Is God Inviting Us Into?

The Scriptures indicate that God wants to talk with us. He has spoken to us from the beginning. He stands at the door of our lives, wanting in, knocking, knocking, and knocking. We see this in the stories of Gideon, Eli, Moses, and Saul of Tarsus. God approached each of these men and talked one-on-one with them; none of them approached him first.

I talk to God all day long, usually about events and challenges. I sometimes wonder if I should pray for a parking spot when some mother in the Sudan is praying that her child won't die. I have two friends who survived the killings in Rwanda. They were forced to flee their homes, and they hid under the floor of a building for a week until the killing stopped. They told stories of many Christians praying for protection, even while their family was being chopped to death. I may be off-roading a bit here, but don't you worry about Christians who claim that God answered their prayer for a new car or lake house? It could be that these luxuries are God's blessing in one's life, but to talk this way is frivolous. It is demeaning to God. To propose that he answers the prayer of a businessman to acquire a new Lexus he doesn't need but denies the desperate mother's prayer to save her child is preposterous.

So what kind of relationship is God inviting us to have with him? Jesus claimed to be friends with his disciples (see John 15:15). Of course, there was the caveat that they do what he told them to do. Is being a friend of God like being with a friend simply because you like each other? Or does "friend of God" fall into the same category as "friend of a president" or some other powerful or famous person? You can be part of the entourage if you pay homage. Do we have to pay proper homage to God?

Some people propose that Jesus is a best friend—that we can "hang" with him, take long walks together on the beach, look in store windows, and talk about which outfit he thinks we should buy. I'm not so sure. Do you really think Jesus has an opinion about your clothes? He may care if you buy a particular piece of clothing, but I doubt very much that he cares about the color. I can't imagine that this is the kind of friendship he desires with us. Is being with Jesus-God so casual, so benignly trivial? I know some will now protest, "How dare you make fun of my relationship with Christ!" It seems as though Jesus wanted to affirm to his followers in the Upper Room that he liked them, that they were friends. But friendship with God is different than friendship with humans. He is not like us, so it makes sense that our relationship with him would be different than our relationship with, say, Jerry, my long-time friend who may burp or something worse at any moment. God is separate; he is different. And he is to be revered, feared, respected. He says, "If any of you wants to be my follower, you must turn from your selfish ways" (Luke 9:23).

How Would You Describe Your Friendship with God?

We feel most comfortable and secure around those friends who accept us for who we are. When that's the case, we don't feel as if we have to hide anything or pretend to be different than we are. We trust these friends and feel comfortable around them. We like being with them. This is friendship at its best.

I was recently reminded that not all friendships are like this. On one of my trips, a church leader picked me up at the airport. After just a few minutes, he started voicing his concerns about his pastor. He spoke of the congregation's decline, of many faithful families who had chosen to leave the church. He said that attendance was down and money was scarce. He said he was the pastor's close friend and that they met weekly. He had even purchased a health-club membership for the pastor so they could work out together and spend time together in a relaxed, informal setting. He said he even wanted to take his pastor friend skiing. Then he began to vent about the mistakes the pastor had made and said that he spoke with his friend about his concerns every time they met. Then he went on to wonder why he couldn't get closer to the pastor. "Why won't he let me into his inner life?" he lamented. I thought I knew the answer, but first I wanted to consult with the pastor himself.

The pastor told me that he was trying his best to be with this man who was courting his most intimate thoughts but that something in his spirit straight-armed the man. The pastor said he didn't trust him. He wasn't sure that the man was on his side. He suspected that he had his own agenda. After listening to the pastor, I got back to the frustrated wealthy "church boss." I told him that he couldn't buy intimacy through gifts and that there was little chance he could get close to the pastor, no matter how much time they spent together. I believed the relationship was doomed to failure. When he demanded to know why, I said, "Because he will never be able to relax and trust you, because you don't accept him. He knows your objective is to fix him. It's not a true friendship if the relationship is one person fixing the other."

Perhaps the most difficult kind of friend is the one who takes from you, who expects a lot from you, but rarely gives back or shows appreciation. There is also the needy friend. Not needy in the sense that something went wrong and you helped that person until he or she got better. No, I am talking about those who are needy by character because they have unmet needs. Chronically needy friends attach themselves to you and suck the life out of you. They show up at the most inconvenient times and want to spend time with you. They get you into projects you don't have time for and that you don't want to do, but do anyway because you don't want to hurt these friends and are afraid that if you do, they will go home and hurt themselves. Some needy friends are unable to support themselves financially due to bad habits or misfortune. My wife and I have had a series of these kinds of friends over the years. For example, there was the neighbor living in a one-room house with ten cats, a dog, a gerbil, and a bird. This all went with no job, no car, and vet bills, and so on. We helped her as we could, even when we shouldn't have. One day she disappeared when she met another "feeder." Like her cats, her loyalty went to the feeder. Jesus says that when we help the person in need, we are helping him. (Common sense will tell you when helping would mean you are enabling evil and when you are really helping your friend.)

I don't know about you, but I think I can be a better friend to God. At times I've been the chronically needy friend who is always on the take from God, wanting to know what's in this relationship for me. Yes, I can definitely be a better friend to God. I want to become the kind of friend to Jesus that he would enjoy being around, someone who is not always asking for something. And I would like to get to the point where I can be with God and not think, *He's trying to fix me*, because such thoughts either make me avoid him or keep me on guard when I am with him.

So can we get to the place where we can relax with Jesus? Where we can trust him and be convinced that he isn't trying to fix us? What will it take to have a true friendship with him?

An Important Ground Rule

The first thing that comes to mind is a principle: We can't be a friend with a pianist if we don't like his playing, nor can we be close to a singer if we don't like her voice. Nor can we be a friend of God's if we always disagree with him about the way he has gone about things. That's the lesson we learn from Job. It is worth noting that God allowed Job to complain; he listened to every word of Job's lament, even when Job cursed the day he was born. But look at where Job arrives after spewing out the pain that was deep within him:

Then the LORD said to Job,

"Do you still want to argue with the Almighty?
    You are God's critic, but do you have the answers?"

Then Job replied to the LORD,

"I am nothing—how could I ever find the answers?
    I will cover my mouth with my hand.
I have said too much already.
    I have nothing more to say." (40:1-5)

All the anger, all the pain, all the confusion, all the sense of betrayal—Job spit it up. He choked on it; there was nothing left inside to get out. It is as though Job never stopped praying, never stopped talking with God. But the final answer was a matter of logic. Job realized who God was and who he was, and that settled the matter. We need to do the same. I have a friend who has decided not to follow Jesus. If every time we get together I insist on revisiting the religious discussion, then I am trying to change my friend. I have not accepted him for who he is. And that is insulting and painful to any relationship; in fact, it will be a reason to avoid each other. It works the same in our relationship with God. Unless we accept God for who he is, then we'll begin to avoid him altogether.

There is one image that has helped me relax around God. I am having dinner with God and other close friends. All of us feel accepted. We are laughing and making fun of each other. Jesus is amused by the banter. He shakes his head when my negative characteristics are brought to light. I can tell by the look on his face that he enjoys me, accepts me, and knows that I am getting more like him. I feel affirmed, even in my weakness. I draw this image from the Revelation 3:20

invitation and from the encounter of Peter and Jesus in John chapter 21, the "Feed my sheep" episode. It is also strengthened by Jesus' patience with his disciples on many occasions, particularly his teaching on servant leadership in Mark 10:35-45. I consider prayer to be God and me talking about what we are doing together: *Today, Lord, we are taking care of the grandson . . . we are celebrating forty years of marriage to my wife . . . we are having an MRI . . . we are teaching some pastors.* God and I are working together, side by side. He is for me; he truly is with me.

Are Appointments Necessary?

Quiet time has long been an expectation that has been promoted to Christians, young and old. For some it has been the source of much joy and accomplishment, but for most it is a millstone around the neck because most people are not disciplined. Consistency requires discipline. Setting and keeping an appointment with God is a habit. I suspect that 90 percent of disciples struggle with this. They feel guilty about their inconsistency and consider it a major failure of their lives.

From my earliest days as a Christ follower, I was told I needed to set a time daily to be with God. If I kept the appointment, then I had been with him. If I missed, I hadn't been with him. I now realize that an either/or approach is not healthy because it is not true. Not only that, it causes self-loathing: "I must not want to be with God enough, not like those superior saints who yearn for those early hours of the morning communing with God with a cup of piping hot coffee."

Being with God is a function that is both divine and human. It is divine in that God is everywhere; he is all-knowing. Nothing is out of his sight or understanding. For that reason, he is with us at all times. Ideally, we are to have an open line of communication with him, an ongoing conversation. That is what it means to be practicing the presence of God. He is always available. Because our friends are not, we usually need to make an appointment to see them.

On the other hand, because we are human, I think it helps to undergird this existential relationship with appointed times of hearing from God through the Scriptures. The only healthy way to do this is to rip your prayer and Bible reading from the hands of legalism. Take your relationship with God and run. Run from the moralists, those who tell you that the more time you log with God in a certain way, the more accepted and spiritual you are. Run from those who tell you that you've heard from God only when tears are found upon the pages of your Bible. Run from those who champion a rigid monasticism that uses self-denial as a means to making you feel better about yourself. And run from those who propose that you are free from any responsibility or discipline in connection to knowing God. Leave both extremes behind; find the healthy place modeled so beautifully by Christ himself.

Now to another important question.

How Does Being with God Make You Feel?

This question could be considered heresy in that it sounds like subjective psychobabble. But let me assure you: the Word of God is true, whether I believe it or not, whether I experience it or not. Therefore, what God is like is not dependent on my personal feelings about him, which are based on my needs. But the question remains, *How does being with God make you feel?* This is important because you will stop meeting with someone if you don't feel you are benefiting from it.

My answer to this question has changed over the years. When I first became a follower of Jesus, I was eager to be with God because others told me I should be. Most public speakers on the subject described emotional interchanges with God. Some even claimed to hear his audible voice. As I understood it, to meet God meant to be told to do something big for him or to be given a special message for the church. Many of the speakers I heard described an aura, a light coming down out of heaven. So I believed being with God was an event that would make me feel important, humble, empowered, confident—a vast array of emotions. A faculty member at my university recruited my room-mate and me to meet with him regularly so that he could help us learn to study the Bible and memorize Scripture. On Saturday mornings, we would go to his house, sit by the fire, and eat doughnuts and he would walk us through Romans and have us recite that week's three memory verses. We memorized more than seventy-five verses, most of which I retain to this day, forty years later. I also remember sleeping in and missing the meeting and trying to avoid the professor during the week.

In time my faculty sponsor invited me to speak at special student meetings about the importance of a consistent quiet time. I was pre-sented as a success story, as a person who had faithfully practiced a daily quiet time and was much the better for it. I was faithful; I loved reading the Bible and memorizing Scripture, and I was very eager, very hungry, and very focused. I was learning so much; I felt satisfied with God. But I don't think I enjoyed my time with him. My meetings with him were like being in the Oval Office with the president. I couldn't relax, and when the meeting was over, I felt relieved that I had accom-plished something important and that I was okay with God.

My walk with God was like this for the first seven years of my Christian life. The second phase began when I started preparing ser-mons and attending seminary. At this time, devotions were replaced by study and preparation to teach. I had been warned about merging the devotional with the scholarly but did it anyway since I had limited time and felt pressure to prepare for both the classroom and the pulpit. As a result, I was reading, praying, teaching, and meditating on Scripture but not reflecting on what I was learning. Of course, just knowing what Scripture is saying and teaching it to others can be very nourishing to the soul. It would be disingenuous of me to say that my heart was cold or that God's Word did not shape my life. I felt that God cared about me; he listened to and answered my prayers and directed my life, but I still didn't want to be with him like I did a close friend. My formal times of prayer and meditation were regular, but two or three times in a week.

Some of my best times with God were in the next phase, when I was an author and traveling teacher. During this period, I was out of a normal life routine. I spent a lot of time alone, and on airplanes, and in hotels. I already had a grasp of the message and teaching of Scripture, so when I read the Bible, I wouldn't learn new things. Instead, I was able to spend the time reviewing what I already knew. Reading has always stimulated my mind and my soul. I have read more books than I could count or even remember. Often times I would find reading a Christian book or a biography much more interesting and, frankly, nourishing than the Bible. Like John Wesley, who read, wrote, and prayed as he traveled by horseback or carriage, I was able to have long prayer times, write, and learn while on airplanes. This continues to be one of my favorite treats, despite the travails of contemporary travel.

I also benefited from having to repeat the same material over and over again as I went from place to place. The discipline of repetition is not commonly revered by those not required to do it. The temptation is to present something new and fresh and forget that the reason you were invited is the message God has given you. The message is what the people need, even if you have lost interest. Even though I already know what I am going to say, I need to prepare myself so that I will practice what I preach. The days that are most difficult are those when I'm speaking to a group of ministers and hear words come out of my mouth that I went against the previous evening. The belief that a spiritual leader must have a life in total alignment with his teaching was dismissed as heresy centuries ago. I keep talking because I know what I am saying is right, even though I have not practiced it. In those moments, I am under a barrage of emotions—humility, guilt, fear, and an overwhelming sense of God's grace. I often ask, *Who is that I hear talking?* I am existing in two conscious worlds. In one world I am speaking to a crowd; in the other I am having a conversation with myself saying, *God would shut me up right now if I were operating on merit.* It is during those moments that I think people should stand back so no one else is hurt in case he does decide to end the charade.

Around this time, I began to feel relaxed in God's presence. I felt an increasing delight in being with him. Time spent with him rejuvenated me. God spoke to me with various impressions that in the context of the events of my life were unmistakable. I found it was much more productive to spend longer periods with him a couple of times a week rather than for shorter periods of time daily. As a result, my daily walk with God was much freer and more joy-filled. I was no longer fearful of being scolded. The more rigid approach to spending time with God is often less a relationship and more a duty. It's similar to calling your mother every day because her feelings would be hurt if you didn't. It's done out of obligation rather than desire. The next phase, which I am still experiencing, started with my desire to be with God as a friend. I realize, of course, that God is wholly other and can never be like a human friend. I'm talking about intensity of emotion, about a more relinquished life. I wasn't sure what I wanted, but I decided to pursue being able to dwell on God's presence, listen to his voice, and focus on his beauty and taste of his goodness. I realize that this may sound a bit feminine to some. In fact, it did to me too, but I sensed it was something to be explored,[1] and I have not been disappointed. I sought and received a sense that God is accepting of me, that he is interested in me as a person, a friend, rather than as someone who works for him. I gained through events in my fifties and now early sixties that the joy of life is found in resting in God's ability to make my life meaningful. When I was freed from the spirit of hurry, of having to make something happen, joy took over, and now I am content when I am with God. I want to be with him, but that doesn't mean I make and keep an appointment every day. I do so several times a week, but I am released to spend this time while walking, working, sitting in a meeting, or driving in my car. When I made this transition, I found the Bible to be revolutionary. Karl Barth is reported to have said, "I have read many books, but the Bible reads me." When I learned to read the Bible reflectively — to read it, to obey it, to confess, to apply it to my life — the revolution began. Today I am living a relationship with God that feels very personal; I am not just claiming to have one by faith.

The needed arrangement with God is very personal. I spend a lot of my time reading the Bible, thinking about the Bible, and preparing myself to teach the Bible. I also read a great many books about Christian faith, so more information is not my need. However, the vast majority of Christ followers are in need of more information and of being reminded of what has been forgotten, because their vocations allow only a few minutes a day for reading and contemplation. They may need a sermon, a home Bible study, and a couple of reading opportunities in a week to be strengthened in their faith. Another person might need to be among people more often in order to make their already-hefty understanding of God alive and relevant. At some point, however—and this has happened to me in this latter stage of formation—the Bible becomes food. You put down your pen and paper and take up your knife and fork. We'll talk more about this in the next chapter.

Reflections

In this chapter, we have moved into the very center of spiritual transformation. After all, being with God is the central theme of all aspects of salvation. This life is about reconciliation and closing the distance. In eternity, the distance disappears. This life has much more promise than what most disciples experience. We have the prospect of being God's friend and of developing the friendship through reflecting on his Word and learning to hear his voice. Living close to God won't keep us from making mistakes, nor will it eliminate suffering, but it is what God created us for: the most abundant of lives.

CHAPTER 8

Reading His Word

When I sit down most mornings to read my Bible, I picture myself entering into an interactive relationship. I expect to be spoken to, and when that happens, God's Word enters my being and I taste it. I love the image so wonderfully presented by Eugene Peterson in his work *Eat This Book*.[1] He utilizes the scene from Revelation of Saint John eating a book, which contains the seven seals that will be opened and will bring history to a close. The book is sweet because it will end evil and vindicate the righteous. But it is also bitter because it will be a bloody and torturous end to the planet.

> I went to the angel and told him to give me the small scroll. "Yes, take it and eat it," he said. "It will be sweet as honey in your mouth, but it will turn sour in your stomach!" So I took the small scroll from the hand of the angel, and I ate it! It was sweet in my mouth, but when I swallowed it, it turned sour in my stomach. (Revelation 10:9-10)

John ate the book; it metabolized in him. It made him feel; it made him happy; it made him sad; it gave him pleasure; it made him sick to his stomach. It has the same effect on us today. My neighbor is reading the Bible. He is flabbergasted with the violence, the crazy people, and the even crazier things they did. Some passages inspire him; others horrify him. He says that some passages are X-rated. But there is no denying that reading God's Word is having an effect on him. It is an experience. He is eating the book, taking it in, and allowing it to have its way. This is how the Bible is intended to be read. We are to put down pen and notebook and take up knife and fork. The Word of God is food. The Word of God is to be taken in, tasted, chewed, savored, swallowed, and digested.

Millions of people read the Bible every day, but getting the Scriptures into people's lives is not easy. Eugene Peterson put it this way: "The challenge—never negligible—regarding the Christian Scriptures is getting them read, but read on their own terms as God's revelation."[2] Bibles are ubiquitous, easy to be found in almost any bookstore and free for the taking in many hotels. Old dusty copies sit around most homes. Getting one isn't much of a challenge, at least in the United States. "What is neglected is reading the Scriptures formatively, reading in order to live."[3] Reading the Scriptures formatively means in a way that changes you. The Bible is a book that requires some intellect and study to grasp, but it is also food for the soul.[4]

Graduation from Exegesis

There is in a sense a graduation from exegesis, an exercise that forms the foundation of our understanding of the Bible, to the school of the Holy Spirit, where Jesus gives instruction. I must be careful here, for a person cannot with safety and confidence go into a more reflective reading of Scripture unless it is based on a solid foundation of biblical exegesis. Exegeting the scriptural text is essential to understanding its message. Knowledge of history, geography, language, culture, customs, and the biography of the writers is a must. This job of exegesis is largely in the hands of scholars and pastors, which is one of the reasons for attending church and attaching oneself to its community. Most people need help in order to be schooled in the Bible's message.

On the inside cover of my Bible, I have written the words "Exegesis is an act of sustained humility." It is the basic work of understanding the meaning of the text. We never master the text; we study it in order to submit to it. From there we can then read Scripture on a deeper and more personal level without violating the authorial intent. There is no deeper meaning inside what the author meant, but there is deeper understanding as it intersects our life experience.

Some may wonder, *Is deeper understanding of the text really an option, or is it a fool's errand?* After all, last night I saw Deepak Chopra interviewed on television about his new book about Jesus. It was an exercise of sophistry that I have not witnessed in some time. Through his reflections on Scripture, he has concocted a picture of Jesus that sends the informed mind reeling. Chopra presented Jesus as one-dimensional, as being primarily about peace and serenity. Chopra seems like a nice-enough man with noble motives, but he mangled the biblical text. That is what can happen when a person lacks a solid foundation of biblical exegesis. This kind of subjectivism keeps Bible believers away from a more reflective life. The primary danger is finding something between the lines of Scripture that contradicts the plain meaning of the text. But that danger aside, I believe that it is worth the effort to explore new dimensions of the spiritual life through the reflective reading of Scripture. This is not about new and special knowledge that changes the Bible's core message; it is about specific insights that relate to a person's life.

Jesus promised,

When the Father sends the Advocate as my representative—that is, the Holy Spirit—he will teach you everything and will remind you of everything I have told you. (John 14:26)

When the Spirit of truth comes, he will guide you into all truth. He will not speak on his own but will tell you what he has heard. He will tell you about the future. He will bring me glory by telling you whatever he receives from me. All that belongs to the Father is mine; this is why I said, "The Spirit will tell you whatever he receives from me." (16:13-15)

The Teacher will remind us of everything Christ taught. He will guide us into truth, he will reinforce what we already know and redirect us when we are in error, and whatever God gives to the Son will be passed along to us. This might be what Jesus promised when he said, "I have come that they may have life, and have it to the full" (John 10:10, NIV).

A Core Course in the Reflective Life

When Willow Creek Community Church commissioned a study of their church along with hundreds of others, they discovered that not much has changed in two thousand years. More than 87 percent of the eighty thousand people surveyed said that understanding the Bible was their first priority. But the finding was even more specific: Those who had reached maturity said that reading the Scriptures in a reflective manner was the main reason they had grown.[5]

Reflective reading of Scripture is uncommon among evangelicals. The emphasis has been on reading and studying for understanding, to know the Bible. The prevailing premise for more than a century has been that knowing the contents of the Bible equals spiritual maturity. Bible knowledge, as I have already stipulated, is essential to knowing God, for serving him and living the life to which he has called us. Sadly, this is where much of the church left it: in our heads but not our hearts. That is why there has been a stampede of interest in the spiritual disciplines, especially with respect to going deeper into Scripture. The words of Saint Bonaventure come to mind: "To know much and taste nothing—of what use is that?"[6]

We enter this school when we begin to read Scripture reflectively. A time-tested method is called *lectio divina*, or divine reading. Some have an immediate knee-jerk reaction to this idea, believing that anything with roots in non-Reformation Christianity (especially in counter-Reformation personnel such as Ignatius of Loyola or any other Catholic monastic leader) is to be rejected. Some Christians can't seem to negotiate that a Catholic might have something of value to say. Even if one might have major problems with Catholic theology, there are many devout followers of Jesus among Catholics who can teach us a great deal about spending time with God. I am not talking about hair shirts, self-flagellation, or other misguided ideas. But one might remember that before the Reformation, almost all Christians were Catholic. Augustine, for whom the book of Romans was such a turning point, was a bishop in the Catholic Church. You can't read his *Confessions* without seeing yourself. Athanasius—who grandly said about the Psalms, "Most scriptures speak to us; Psalms speak for us"[7]—is another. I don't need to agree with Saint Thomas Aquinas and Thomas à Kempis in order to appreciate some of their work. Only theological hubris would dismiss the lot. After all, it was the monastics who saved Western Christianity and held it in trust for five hundred years in convents and monasteries. Christianity would have collapsed without literacy and sacred documents. One of the monastics' finer contributions was reflective reading and meditation on Scripture. Again, keep in mind that this is to be done on a foundation of sound biblical exegesis.

Lectio Divina

Lectio divina has four movements:

Lectio. First, select a Scripture passage, take a short section, and then with a listening heart read the text aloud, slowly and deliberately. When you find a word or phrase or sentence that speaks to your heart, pause in your reading.

Meditatio. Second, meditate or mull over the word or words. Allow God to settle the word into your soul. Allow it to probe your attitude, emotions, and aspirations.

Oratio. Third, return the Scripture you have just read to the

Father by praising him for its work in you. Talk to the Father about your reading.

Contemplatio. The final stage is resting in the Lord's presence. This is the act of simply being with God.[8]

I prefer to simplify and bring it down to earth by adopting what can be found in the study version of *The Message*:

Lectio. Read it. Read it slowly, over and over.

Meditatio. Think it. What does it mean? What does it say? Do I have the primary meaning of the words in my head?

Oratio. Pray it. Pray the words, interact with God, and ask the Holy Spirit to teach you the special applications for your life.

Contemplatio. Live it. Review your immediate life, attitudes, and conflicts. Ask yourself, *How does this relate to my schedule, appointments, and challenges this very day?*

Reflective reading of Scripture also includes memorization of it.

Memorization of Scripture

People in general claim to have memory problems. The older we get, the more difficulty we have memorizing anything, and that includes Scripture. Some have benefited by memorization techniques. I know I have when I have needed to recall information for an exam or give a sermon. But without doubt, the most valuable memorization in my life has been of the Scriptures. Because it is encouraged in the Bible, I believe it is something that God through His Spirit helps us with. I would submit that Scripture memory is possible when other kinds of memorization might be nearly impossible.

And the purpose for memorizing Scripture? "I have hidden your word in my heart, that I might not sin against you" (Psalm 119:11). Countless times I have been saved from sin because I called upon Scripture to strengthen me. Temptation can be very strong. I have held on by my spiritual fingernails over many a steep cliff by remembering this verse: "The temptations in your life are no different from what others experience. And God is faithful. He will not allow the temptation to be more than you can stand. When you are tempted, he will show you a way out so that you can endure" (1 Corinthians 10:13).

Always Submit to the Text

Eugene Peterson warns us about using the Bible for our personal gain, whether it be intellectual, practical, or inspirational.[9] It's possible to know all the history, languages, culture, and geography of the Bible yet be satisfying only your intellectual needs. This is most common among teachers and pastors, those who love an intellectual feast. It's also possible to approach Scripture as simply a handbook for living. You may have heard such pragmatists bellow, "If the Scriptures don't work, they don't matter." These folks are looking for tips to becoming more successful; they want to ramp up their businesses or multiply their resources. Others come to Scripture simply for inspiration; they just want to feel better. All these motivations are very human and very much using the Bible for one's own purpose. But what's missing is submission to the text and the willingness to do what it says. So the warning is to be committed to obedience.

Eugene Peterson summarizes for us:

> *Lectio divina* is not a methodical technique for reading the Bible. It is a cultivated developed habit of living the text in Jesus' name. This is the way, the only way, that the Holy Scriptures become formative in the Christian church and become salt and leaven in the world.[10]

Reflections

One of the benefits of thinking about developing good habits is to remember the practices of the ancient church. What the Reformation took away from many of our traditions is the unity of the seven major practices of the church. The first was communion, the second tithing, and the third fasting. These have largely survived the divide between Protestant and Catholic.

The next four major practices have been lost to many. The fourth was the hours of the day that the church would pray. The church would, according to Jewish tradition, pray six times a day. Prayer would be at six, nine, noon, three, six, and at retiring. This was the practice of the early church; they would just stop and pray for a minute or two. The fifth practice was the Sabbath, a time of rest and reflection. The sixth was the church year or calendar, which would condition a person to experience the steps of redemption, incarnation, preparation for the passion of Christ, his death, his resurrection, his ascension, and the sending of the Holy Spirit at Pentecost. The last ancient practice was pilgrimage, where once in a lifetime a Christian goes to a special place to pay homage and for reflection. It doesn't need to be a Holy Land tour; it could be to your family home or to visit significant friends who have contributed to your spiritual life. There is power in structure and tradition.

Even though I am not particularly traditional, I see the value in these ancient practices and how they assist us in knowing God more personally.

CHAPTER 9

Hearing His Voice

A sign of psychosis, a term for losing touch with reality, is the hearing of voices. The celluloid images of Sally Field in *Sybil* and Jessica Lange in *Frances* as well as the demented smile of Jack Nicholson in *One Flew Over the Cuckoo's Nest* have been fixed in the public psyche. Quintessential mental illness is a person curled up in the fetal position in a mental hospital, hands over the ears, screaming—begging—for the voices to stop. Chief among the voices they hear is God's. But the mentally ill aren't the only ones claiming to hear God's voice.

Religious people also claim to hear from God. Some are leaders of cults. Thirty years ago, Jim Jones evoked the voice of God to lead nine hundred people to drink a juice laced with poison so they could commit mass suicide. The Jonestown tragedy was the origin of the phrase "They drank the Kool-Aid," which is used in reference to any group who mindlessly follows a leader. More recent examples include David Koresh and the Branch Davidians and Warren Jeffs and his Mormon-like cult. All of these men did evil in the name of hearing God's voice. Many televangelists also claim to hear the voice of God. They say that because God speaks to them, they know stuff the common Christian does not and that is why they should be listened to and we should send them money: so they can influence God to help us with their unique connection to the Almighty. They believe they are special, and so they incarnate the prosperity message by living an extravagant lifestyle. It is much like Robert Altman's film *Gosford Park*, where the elite are catered to 24/7. They must drive the best automobiles, unless they are being chauffeured in them, and fly on private aircraft. The most obvious extravagances are the two-thousand-dollar suits and dresses. There are also the gaudy rings, necklaces, and earrings and the professionally coiffed hair, tinted just so for television, usually with an unintended orange or purple glow. I especially enjoy the jet-black hair against a seventy-five-year-old's pasty skin. If this is what God has done for fashion, I serve a God with poor taste. I marvel at how God's speaking to you can cause such unseemly behavior.

Because we are all aware of people who've committed crimes and abuse in the name of hearing God's voice, it's easy to be suspect of anything outside the written document of God's Word. But does that mean God speaks to us only through his Word?

Does God Still Speak?

The year I became a Christ follower, I became a student at Oral Roberts University. The university had been open for just two years, but it already had become a major tourist attraction in the state of Oklahoma. The buildings looked like something out of *Star Trek*; you expected to see Captain Kirk and Spock walking the corridors of the buildings. The gymnasium looked like a spaceship, an administration and classroom building was held up by golden columns, and at the center of campus stood a hundred-foot, ten-story prayer tower that looked as if it might take off at any moment.

I remember listening as Oral Roberts stood before the student body and told us the story of ORU. One day in the early 1960s, he was walking on the land where the university stands and God told him, "Build me a university," which he did. God also told Roberts, "Take my healing power to your generation," which he did as well. ORU now stands as the premier Charismatic institution of learning in the United States. I have never been sure why God needed a university after seeing what happened with Harvard, Princeton, Yale, and other schools that started out to do his will. He later told Pat Robertson and Jerry Falwell to build him a university too. Oral Roberts also claims that God told him to build the City of Faith, which at one time housed a law school, medical school, and hospital. The three towers now called CityPlex are partially rented and a constant financial drain on the university. Roberts claims he saw a nine-hundred-foot Jesus figure that directed him in this now-discredited venture. On a previous occasion, God reportedly told Roberts that if he didn't get eleven million dollars by a certain date, his work would be done and God might as well call him home. What is not reported is that the eleven million did arrive on time. I suppose we could say that Oral Roberts was batting .500; he was two for four on God's speaking to him.

God does speak, even in an audible voice, but at times our need to hear his voice causes us to imagine that he has spoken clearly when in fact he has not. Scripture tells us that God spoke to Adam, Cain, Abel, Noah, Abraham, Moses, Gideon, and many others in history. But does he speak now to normal disciples, those of us to whom he may never speak audibly and to whom he does not give a spectacular assignment?

What Did Jesus Actually Promise?

Jesus posited himself as the Good Shepherd. There are certain qualities he attributed to his relationship with his flock:

> The gatekeeper opens the gate for him, and *the sheep recognize his voice* and come to him. He calls his own sheep by name and leads them out. After he has gathered his own flock, he walks ahead of them, and they follow him because *they know his voice.* They won't follow a stranger; they will run from him because *they don't know his voice.* . . . I am the good shepherd; I know my own sheep, and they know me. . . . *They will listen to my voice,* and there will be one flock with one shepherd. (John 10:3-5,14,16, emphasis added)

Four times Jesus claims that his people will know his voice and follow him, just as sheep recognize their shepherd's voice and trust him.

Folks marvel when they observe voice-recognition software on display. Someone can sit at a computer and merely speak and the words appear on a screen. But isn't it even more amazing that a blind person can know every person around him or her easily by the voice-recognition instrument that comes factory installed in every person? When someone who hasn't contacted us in a while calls, it just takes a moment and we recognize his or her voice.

But because God rarely speaks to us audibly, how can we recognize his voice? After all, we don't want to be like Rex Humbard, who claimed that God told him to build a huge tower to his glory in Akron, Ohio. Sadly for Rex and for Akron, Rex ran out of money. The core of the tower was finished, but the revolving restaurant on top was not. To this day, it stands tall over the city of Akron, a testament to Rex Humbard's ego. So how can we know when God truly is speaking directly to us?

How God Speaks to Us

Most of us don't have any trouble knowing if God is speaking to us from Scripture. However, a single passage must be understood in the context of the overall teaching of the Bible. For example, if someone reads that in Christ there is no difference between male or female, Jew or Gentile, slave or free (see Galatians 3:28), it doesn't mean that what the Scriptures teach about the submission of authority for men and women in marriage or the distinction between Jews and Gentiles in other parts of Scripture is to be disregarded. As Dallas Willard has said,

> A single statement directly from the Bible—and these are so
> often invoked for personal guidance—may be used contrary
> to the purposes of God, contrary to any meaning that he may

have in mind for us. That is why it is only the Bible as a whole that can be treated as the written Word of God.[1]

Entire books have been written on the subject of hearing God's voice. The best of the lot is Dallas Willard's *Hearing God*; it may be the most profound of his works.

Most people I know who are listening to God consider his voice an inner voice—a prompting, an impression, an inner urge that won't go away. Paul, who had heard God's audible voice on several occasions, spoke of the more normative means of communication in this way: "God is at work in you, both to will and to work for his good pleasure" (Philippians 2:13, RSV). The words of interest are "to will." God "wills" things in us, and most often this is an interior experience. When people say, "God spoke to me," they usually mean it in a colloquial way; they are saying that God impressed something on them.

My first such experience with this was while I was on a student mission in East Africa in 1968. I had been asked to give a sermon to about seventy villagers. I didn't consider myself a preacher, but I gave the sermon through an interpreter, and the entire group indicated they wanted to follow Jesus. As I stood in an open field in Kenya, God spoke to me. The inner voice said, "This is what you are to do." God's voice wasn't audible, but it didn't need to be; it was clear and convincing. I haven't questioned it since. The circumstances set the stage. Without the context, I probably would have ignored the inner voice.

For many years now I have been an advocate of F. B. Meyer and his explanation of God speaking to us.[2] He wrote,

> God's impressions within and his word without are always corroborated by his providence around, and we should quietly wait until those three focus into one point. If you do not know what you ought to do, stand still until you do. And when the time comes for action, circumstances, like glowworms, will sparkle along your path; and you will become so sure that you

are right, when God's three witnesses concur, that you could not be surer though an angel beckoned you on.[3]

Meyer's three lights are: circumstances, impressions from the Spirit, and passages from the Bible. I think of it as seeing three separate lights in the distance. When all three merge into one light, God has spoken.

Most of us don't struggle with the clear voice of Scripture or even circumstances when they nicely coincide with what the Bible seems to be saying. The tricky part is the inner voice, the "impressions," because we may have heard that still small voice that makes us feel smaller still. The inner voices we hear can be castigating, rude, and downright depressing, so what is the character of God's voice?

The Character of His Voice

Sometimes I get an impression that God wants me to talk to someone about something: "Go talk to that person" or "Call Fred." I usually don't respond immediately to these urges. One day I was standing in front of a restaurant, waiting for my appointment, when a man rolled by in a wheelchair. I had an urge to go up to him and ask him if he wanted to be healed, that I should lay hands on him and try to lift him out of the wheelchair. I almost did but lost my courage (or came to my senses; I'm not sure which). At times, I wonder if I would live on a much higher plain if I gave in to these impulses. To do so is risky. I could be considered unstable if I obeyed this inner voice and things went wrong. In 1969, I told a young man who was paraplegic that God was going to heal him and that he would walk again. I prayed for him, unstrapped him from the chair, and tried to lift him out. He flopped back in the chair all three times I lifted him. Might it be possible for me to get to a place of discernment, where I am able to avoid the embarrassing and kooky behavior and actually break through into people's lives?

Experience is a part of recognizing God's voice, but as we've seen, some dangerous and bizarre happenings can take place if divine voice recognition is not grounded in a more objective realm. Dallas Willard suggests there are three characteristics: quality of voice, spirit of voice, and content of voice.[4]

The Quality of the Voice

The quality of God's voice is always authoritative; it is never irritating, whining, or cold. E. Stanley Jones, a Methodist missionary statesman, wrote this about how to distinguish the voice of God from our own subconscious:

> Perhaps the rough distinction is this: The Voice of the subconscious argues with you, tries to convince you; but the inner voice of God does not argue, does not try to convince you. It just speaks and it is self-authenticating. It has the feel of the voice of God within it.[5]

Jones' reflections seem accurate when we consider Adam, Cain, Abraham, Moses, and others. None of them wondered who was speaking. The sound of God's voice is unmistaken when it is audible.

Very few claim to hear the audible voice of God. If I heard someone make this claim, I would be suspicious and want to test the veracity of the message. I would ask, *Does the message strengthen the entire church?* So often what passes for God's voice is purely devoted to promotion of a personal agenda, and self-aggrandizing to boot.

The Spirit of the Voice

James wrote,

> The wisdom from above is first of all pure. It is also peace loving, gentle at all times, and willing to yield to others. It is full of mercy and good deeds. It shows no favoritism and is always sincere. (3:17)

This goes back to the idea that God will not demean you; he will not accuse you. He will speak in the Spirit of Jesus. I don't want to diminish the authority of Jesus. You might remember his confrontational manner in opposition to the Pharisees—the names he called them and the anger he displayed. He was uncompromising and condemning.[6] I've always considered a lively study to be one that reviews passages in which Jesus was mad. Such a study reveals what God considers to be the real enemy, Satan, with whom we are locked in battle. So when I say that God's voice will always be affirming, I don't mean it will always be sugarcoated. It may bear some mention of accountability and areas of improvement, but it will always be encouraging, I believe, to those whose hearts are turned God's way. Some of the most encouraging people in my life have affirmed their belief in me while at the same time mentioning areas needing attention.

Of course, we can get this all mixed up and not be sure if God is speaking to us. This is when patience and counsel are needed. Years ago I was undecided about whether I should take a new position. It was an attractive offer, and many had recommended me for the position, but it required a move for my family, and it was not a pastoral position. Every pastor knows what I mean when I say that leaving the pastorate for another job can be traumatic. You hear those voices: *Oh, you're leaving the ministry* or *Why would you leave the teaching of the Bible? That is your gift. After all, you were called to preach.* Another voice went something like this: *If you go to a denominational position, you might be considered a bureaucrat and your reputation as a Bible teacher may suffer or even go away.* My wife said only one thing: "If you take this, make sure it is God; otherwise we will have a tough time." That, my friends, is pressure.

One night as I was returning home from a meeting, I was praying, asking God for some help, a sign, anything to end the misery of indecision. Then I saw it, a huge billboard high above me. It was lit bright against the black sky: "Go for it." That was all it said, and I just knew it was for me. Remember Meyer's three lights? Circumstances, impressions from the Spirit, and passages of Scripture? This was that inner voice, with the help of a prop, that spoke clearly to me. If there had been no prop and the words had been written in the night sky, I am sure I would have driven off the road. It was the last piece of the puzzle that nudged me over the decisional line. I took the job, and it was a wonderful experience, some of my very best years. The Spirit of the voice was the Holy Spirit, and it gave me the belief that I could do the job, like a coach giving me a pat on the back and sending me into the game, saying, "You can do it, kid."

The Content of the Voice

The content of the voice is another key. The basic rule is that the content must match God's written Word and conform to the truths about God's nature. I should point out that there have been many times that what people say they heard from God did meet this test yet didn't turn out to be wisdom. God speaks to us in principles more than in particulars:

> It is the principles, not the incidentals of scripture, that count here. Study of the scriptures makes it clear that there are certain things that are fundamental, absolute and without exception. These elements show up with stunning clarity as we become familiar with the overall content of scripture.[7]

Here are three guidelines for evaluating whether the content of the message is from God: Put principles over specific passages, sort out thoughts and perceptions, and beware the utopian voice. Let's look at each of these.

1. Put principles over specific passages. People have claimed that God told them to sell all they have because of the story of the rich young ruler. Of course, this is not a common claim, but Saint Antony, reportedly a wealthy Egyptian of the fourth century, heard the story being read in church, and immediately went out and gave his inheritance of land to the townspeople. He sold all he had and gave the money to the poor. He then began his life as a hermit, monk, or desert father. Hundreds of others followed his lead. My caution is the method he used. I believe he made an impulsive decision based upon a particular passage that was not meant to be understood as a general principle of the gospel.

This pitfall can be avoided by living in the principles of Scripture. For example:

- You must love the LORD your God with all your heart, all your soul, and all your mind. (Matthew 22:37)
- A soft answer turns away wrath. (Proverbs 15:1, RSV)
- God is never tempted to do wrong, and he never tempts anyone else. (James 1:13)
- God is faithful. He will not allow the temptation to be more than you can stand. (1 Corinthians 10:13)
- If any of you wants to be my follower, you must turn from your selfish ways, take up your cross daily, and follow me. (Luke 9:23)
- Seek first His kingdom and His righteousness, and all these things will be added to you. (Matthew 6:33, NASB)

These are all general principles that are the basic content of God's wisdom. "Principles of scripture are most of all to be identified from the actions, spirit, and explicit statements of Jesus himself. When we take him in his wholeness as our model and the one to follow—and what else could it mean to trust him? We will safely identify the content of the inner voice of God."[8]

2. Sort out thoughts and perceptions. I don't think most of us are confused by the clear principles of God's Word and subsequently God's nature. We all know that it is his will for us to be kind, forgiving, and loving toward others and to live an orderly life of peace. Circumstances are not confusing in and of themselves. If you are stuck alongside the road with a flat tire in the pouring rain, that is awful but not confusing. But if you are a bride and the flat tire will make you late for your own wedding, you may be confused. *Does this mean God is telling me not to go through with the marriage? Is God speaking to me? Or is this the voice of the Enemy, who is trying to steal a wonderful future from me?* How might you sort through your confusion?

Let us assume for a moment that F. B. Meyer's three lights have come together and confirmed your marriage. You certainly have the blessing of Scripture for the institution of marriage. You have the same feeling that Adam and Eve seemed to have at their first meeting in the Garden of Eden, a feeling of attraction and desire. The circumstances up to now have been positive. Both families have blessed your union, and all the things the families feel are important to a successful marriage are present. The thoughts and impressions thus far have been all systems go. Your inner voices have confirmed this in you. So why are you suddenly, as you sit alongside the road in your five-thousand-dollar wedding dress, in crisis? The Enemy is attacking you with fear—the fear of the future and the uncertainty that comes with a lifelong commitment. His plan is to cause you to miss what God has already confirmed, and he will use normal feelings of uncertainty about the future to destroy a union destined to serve and please God for many years. Satan's voice is that still, small voice that makes you feel smaller still. It makes you feel stupid, like a fool. Don't listen to this voice. It's the Enemy wanting to take you down.

3. Beware the utopian voice. This is the voice that promises you a life of ease, a life exempt from suffering, disease, failure, and setbacks. This voice says that your business will grow without difficulty, your body will remain healthy, and your church will be problem free—that is how you will know God's blessing is on you. If you believe this voice, when problems come, you will be tempted to doubt your faith.

Even as I write these words, a close friend of mine is undergoing a delicate operation for cancer. It is his third major surgery in his forty-four years of life. He is a devoted Christian, father, and husband. He and his wife have served many years as missionaries. This is what they get? Years of suffering and setbacks? If my friend believed the utopian voice, he might think he has sin in his life and that God has removed his blessing from him. This voice is devilish as well and has no place in a Christian's thinking. Lucifer wants us to believe falsehoods about God so that when we do suffer, we lose our faith.

You Will Make Mistakes

Any human will develop misunderstandings and mental confusions about guidance. There will be times when you get it wrong; this, however, should not discourage you from seeking God's pathway. It is so essential to rest your mind and will in the written Word of God. You can't always make the right application or even get the right interpretation, but you can avoid big mistakes by not violating the main tenets of Scripture.

Most mistakes are not created from a misinterpretation of God's general will for a life. They are birthed in the flaws of human personality. My Achilles heel has been impulsiveness; I see the prize and grab it. Impatience joined to impulsiveness is a disaster. Early in our marriage, it became apparent that my wife, Jane, was a controlled shopper. She could go shopping for hours and buy nothing; she just enjoyed the process. I went shopping and came home with a new car or television. I didn't even want to compare with other stores or auto dealers. My motto was "Let's just get it done." If I became excited about a new project in church or product in a store, I was ready to go for it. At home it got me into trouble financially; at church it got me into trouble relationally. This trait had to be trained out of me over many years. It is no longer a chronic part of my personality, but it can still make a special appearance, a reunion tour, when I am unguarded. I can recall many mistakes I have made in my personal and vocational life because I was unable or unwilling to wait on God. The inability to wait on God is a lack of spiritual maturity. This is why we need others so much: They can help us wait.

Regrets are a reality, but they are not a productive course in a person's progress. Repentance, on the other hand, paves the way for spiritual formation, for the change that leaves the destructive parts of our personality behind. Repentance is a work of God's Spirit, in which our opinions about our malfunctions are changed. True repentance includes the desire and the training for the discipline to put off old patterns and replace them with new ones. The need to focus on past mistakes is a pathology endorsed by Satan himself; he is the accuser (see John 10:10; Revelation 12:9)[9] and uses your past to break down your confidence and joy. There is a difference between a Freudian look at our past, which either excuses or explains our present problems, and a redemptive look at our past, which applies the power of Christ to the present issue. Christ uses our past as a springboard. So rather than look back, move forward in repentance. Yes, you have missed the mark and made mistakes in your reading of God's will. Trust God, who is beside you and who continues to lead you with joy and confidence.

Reflections

Living close to God won't eliminate mistakes, suffering, and appearing loony at times, but it is what God created us for. It is the most abundant of lives. Living close to God teaches us about ourselves. I delight in C. S. Lewis's description of his attempt to be meditative:

> During my afternoon "meditations," —which I at least attempt quite regularly now—I have found out ludicrous and terrible things about my own character. Sitting by, watching the rising thoughts to break their necks as they pop up, one learns to know the sort of thoughts that do come. And, will you believe it, one out of every three is a thought of self-admiration: when everything else fails, having had its neck broken, up comes the thought, "What an admirable fellow I am to have broken their

necks!" I catch myself posturing before the mirror, so to speak, all day long. I pretend I am carefully thinking out what to say to the next pupil (for his good, of course) and then suddenly realize I am really thinking how frightfully clever I'm going to be and how he will admire me. . . . And then when you force yourself to stop it, you admire yourself for doing that. It is like fighting the Hydra. . . . There seems to be no end to it. Depth under depth of self-love and self-admiration.[10]

I find this passage helpful in my own struggle to being with God in a meditative state. There is too much emphasis in Christian literature on being with God in the unnatural state of a meditative chamber created by our own ability to shut out the rest of life. The concept of a spiritual discipline is to train ourselves to be more deeply in touch with God. Lewis found the exercise of setting aside time to hear from God very frustrating and very revealing. One gets the idea he didn't enjoy it much. However, he did subject himself to it on a semi-regular basis. It is well known that Lewis attended morning prayer during the week while staying on campus. It is clear from this passage that he also set aside other times in which he struggled but gained something.

I would encourage more emphasis on the natural state of living with God side by side during each day. I think Lewis found walking tours much more conducive to being with God than the "sitting still and trying to shut everything out" routine. Some of you are contemplative personalities; you find it easy to sit and listen quietly for the voice of God. I, like Lewis, find my mind wandering, taking little mental tours, but in the end, I also find these times agonizingly helpful as to my spiritual condition.

CHAPTER 10

The Development of the Spiritual Heart

Most people innately sense that the healthiest form of spirituality is to have a heart to please God and from that heart of passion to respond to him in obedience. The ancients believed that action followed essence, that our actions are consistent with the reality of our hearts. This accounts for the popular belief that good works are of secondary significance to the heart; they are effects rather than causes. The flip side, however, is the fear that if we depend on feelings, passions, and emotions, we will sin, giving in to the powerful self-interest deep within our hearts. We need to take sin seriously. As Reinhold Niebuhr taught Elton Trueblood, "Sin is the precise sense of self-centeredness and the struggle for power."[1] The struggle begins in childhood over toys, friends, and being chosen first in games. This struggle is daily and at the heart of every decision. There is danger and the possibility of disaster when we depend too much on passion or desire. But less passion does not mean less sin, nor does it mean more obedience.

We cast our lot with C. S. Lewis, who addresses the human tendency to play it safe with God:

> If we consider the unblushing promises of reward and the staggering nature of the rewards promised in the Gospels, it would seem that Our Lord finds our desires, not too strong, but too weak. We are half-hearted creatures, fooling about with drink and sex and ambition when infinite joy is offered us, like an

ignorant child who wants to go on making mud pies in a slum because he cannot imagine what is meant by the offer of a holiday at the sea. We are far too easily pleased.[2]

The spiritual heart can be strengthened, its passions made greater. When we engage God in the way he has recommended, we can have a passionate spiritual heart that directs our transformation, that keeps the internal motivation and external behavior in balance. We can have a spiritual heart that brings congruency to all of life.

It is crucial to understand that one does not arrive at such a state by wishing or hoping. Many have experienced spiritual growth as one dream piled upon another dream, followed by disappointment. Who hasn't attended a retreat or special event that led to a passionate desire to change and experience the fullness of God? At the close of such experiences, the renewed passion gives rise to fist pumping and cheer-leading. We naturally desire that the good feeling continue, to not let it waft and wane away. But the powerful emotions always diffuse into the tissue of everyday life. The desire to no longer be abusive to others is only the beginning of the process.

There is a way out of this "New Year's resolution" spirituality. The radical and refreshing thought to all this is that we can become the kind of persons who naturally do what Jesus would do. We can take the emotional power present in us and redirect it into rearranging our lives around the practices of Jesus so that we can form a spiritual heart or character.

What Is the Spiritual Heart?

Before Sigmund Freud and Carl Jung invented psychoanalysis and excavated the soul, reducing it to primal or mystical motives, there was *A System of Biblical Psychology*, published in 1855 by Franz Delitzsch, the renowned Hebrew scholar and commentator. It remains the most thorough work on the immaterial nature of humanity. Delitzsch's treatment of what the Bible calls the "heart" is exhaustive, but here is a good summary of what he says: "The heart is the innermost centre of the natural condition of man, in which the threefold life of man blends together."[3] That threefold part of man is mind, spirit, and body. The "heart denotes also the middle or the centre of natural things. The heart is the centre of the bodily function, it is the reservoir of the entire life force."[4]

Delitzsch describes the ways of the heart as follows:

The heart is the seat of love, of hatred, it knows and perceives, it understands, deliberates, reflects, estimates, is set and directed, it turns away from and is inclined towards, things can be written on the heart, one knows in his heart if he is conscious to himself, the heart is the storehouse of all that is heard and experienced. Because it is the birthplace of the thoughts, the heart is, moreover, the birthplace of words. Words are brought forth from the heart.[5]

Rarely does the Bible refer to the physical organ of the heart. Scriptural references to it are usually a metaphor for the immaterial nature of a person. Paul wrote, "I do not cease to give thanks for you, remembering you in my prayers, that the God of our Lord Jesus Christ, the Father of glory, may give you a spirit of wisdom and of revelation in the knowledge of him, *having the eyes of your hearts enlightened*, that you may know what is the hope to which he has called you, what are the riches of his glorious inheritance in the saints" (Ephesians 1:16-18, RSV, emphasis added). The heart can see, feel, know, reflect, and be turned toward or away from God.

Spiritual formation is the development of a heart for God. That "spiritual heart" directs the transformation of the entire person to reflect Jesus Christ. It denotes a passion and warmth of relationship, one that is current and alive, one in which there is communication—an honest interchange including disappointment, disagreement, forgiveness, and reconciliation. The spiritual heart encompasses the will, the mind, the spirit, feelings, conscience, and other biblical descriptions of the inner person.

Training the Intention of the Heart

A regenerate heart desires to be at one with God and please him (see Ephesians 1:17-18). Some would call the condition of the spiritual heart "character." While most of the discussion about why Christians don't live according to their beliefs centers around character, I would like to present it as a deeper issue, that being the intention of the heart.

William Law's *A Serious Call to a Devout and Holy Life* has changed many lives because of its razor-sharp dissection of the heart's intention. Published in 1728, this powerful work influenced the lives of such spiritual greats as Samuel Johnson and John Wesley. It has had a potent effect on leaders of contemporary Christian thought, such as Dallas Willard and Richard Foster. Law's premise concerning intention is as simple as it is startling. He asks why it is that so many professing Christians live contrary to the principles in which they say they believe. He applies this question to the problem of Christian men swearing in their public life but not in their religious life and concludes that the reason they continue to swear is that they never fully intended not to. Their heart's intent was to hold back, to reserve a part of their lives that they could continue to control. We are in a constant negotiation with God about who is in charge. But a holy and devout life calls for surrender, not negotiation. So we must go into training in order to gradually grow out of the grip of our own corrupted hearts and strengthen our spiritual hearts (see 1 Corinthians 9:24-27).

As we saw in chapter 3, we can have a new heart, one that God has put in us, and at the same time have the deceptive heart. The Bible makes it clear that the heart cannot be fully trusted:

The human heart is the most deceitful of all things,
    and desperately wicked.

Who really knows how bad it is?
But I, the Lord, search all hearts
    and examine secret motives.
I give all people their due rewards,
    according to what their actions deserve.
        (Jeremiah 17:9-10)

Richard Foster describes our inner person this way:

We are, each and every one of us, a tangled mass of motives: hope and fear, faith and doubt, simplicity and duplicity, honesty and falsity, openness and guile. God is the only one who can separate the true from the false, the only one who can purify the motives of the heart.[6]

Can a person's intention change or be changed from a power outside of itself? The answer must be yes or there is no need to continue this discussion. That's why Paul in his Ephesians letter prayed that "the eyes of your hearts [be] enlightened" (1:18, RSV). He prayed that the heart would see more the way God sees. As we experience the good and bad of life, we start seeing life more like God sees it. It is surprising how this change takes place. It is what we call the common, or ordinary, life.

The Common Life

We naturally tend to separate our religious life from our common life. The religious life is attending church services, observing special religious holidays, keeping Advent calendars, and trying not to eat dessert during Lent. It involves daily devotions, going on Christian mission trips, attending a Bible study, helping the poor, and many good things called "Christian." All these activities have intrinsic value, but it is possible to do all of these things and for them to have no effect at all on a person's common life. The common life is how we treat our spouse and children, how we drive our cars, and the media we take in. It is what is going on "under the hood." How does a Christian business leader treat his or her employees? Is he a man of his word? Can she be trusted? It is necessary for disciples of Christ to bring their lives under his direction. A Christian may be attentive to his or her religious life but be ruled by worry, anger, pride, and sensuality in his or her common life. William Law gives us an eighteenth-century view of this problem:

> It is very possible for a man that lives by cheating, to be very punctual in paying for what he buys; but then everyone is assured that he does not do so out of any principle of true honesty. In like manner it is very possible for a man that is proud of his estate, ambitious in his views, or vain of his learning, to disregard his dress and person in such a manner as a truly humble man would do; but to suppose that he does so out of true principle of religious humility, is fully as absurd as to suppose that a cheat pays for what he buys out of a principle of religious honesty.[7]

The real power to affect others is found in the transformation of our inner life and in how it affects the common parts of our experience. Many times we think we have been transformed because our lives have been free from murder, theft, and adultery. How sad that we have accepted the exercise of our religious duties and the absence of public sin that will embarrass us as our definition of transformation. This is what happens when we find a level of religious experience that will allow us to hold on to the core of our flesh in order to maintain control of our lives. This limited view leaves out the pursuit of God, the joys of surrender, and the fullness of a heart so passionate for God that it directs and governs all our attitudes and decisions. When it comes to attitude, William Law once again speaks powerfully around the subject of death:

When we consider death as a misery, we only think of it as a miserable separation from the enjoyments of this life. We seldom mourn over an old man that dies rich, but we lament the young, that are taken away in the progress of their fortune. You yourselves look upon me with pity, not that I am going unprepared to meet the Judge of the quick and dead, but that I am to leave a prosperous trade in the flower of my life. This is the wisdom of our human thoughts. And yet what folly of the silliest children is so great as this?[8]

I think of Charles Spurgeon, who was being given a tour of a very expensive home. As the owner was extolling the Italian marble floors and the Kenyan wood-paneled walls, Spurgeon reportedly said, "These are the things that make it hard to die." Spurgeon was voicing the human tendency to hold on to this life because of a flawed perspective about the next one.

Law eloquently describes the heart that has a surrendered intentionality toward God:

It is so far from being impossible now, that if we can find any Christians that sincerely intend to please God in all their actions, as the best and happiest thing in the world, whether they be young or old, single or married, men or women, if they have but this intention, it will be impossible for them to do otherwise. This one principle will infallibly carry them to this height of love, and they will find themselves unable to stop short of it.[9]

I find these statements riveting. When we have the sincere intention to please God in all our actions, we allow him to dig down deep inside us and to get at the deepest reasons we do what we do. This includes who we are in our common life—the real person we are, not just the public religious person we project. And if we are sincerely intent on pleasing God, we will believe that pleasing him is what will make us happiest and that we are not missing anything when we abstain from sin and pursue pleasing God. The spiritual heart must believe this in order to govern and direct our lives. This is at the core of the development of the spiritual heart. We win over lust when we believe we are not missing anything of value by not lusting. We stop lying when we won't miss the advantage or the benefits of lying. Law's other statements seem too good to be true: that we would find ourselves unable to do otherwise than please God, that we would not be able to stop ourselves. This is because a sincerely intended heart inclined to please God is directing us.

Heart Work

Some believe that heart work is hard work, which makes following Christ easy. But heart work is hard work only in that making ourselves available to God requires discipline. Paul has told us several times and ways, "Discipline yourself for the purpose of godliness" (1 Timothy 4:7, NASB). By discipline, Paul meant the will and structure needed for repeated exercise. This is evident by his mention in the next verse about bodily exercise. That discipline comes from two sources, the Holy Spirit and the fellow members of Christ's body who join with us on the journey. Everyone who has tried to become Christlike alone either gave up or came up short, more malformed than formed. It is the treachery of the human heart that when left to itself, it will disfigure what is actually real and true.

If you submit to the process suggested in the chapters on being with God, reading his Word, and hearing his voice, God will begin to change your heart. We all have the responsibility to act, to "grow in grace" (see 2 Peter 3:18). Christ knocks at the door of our lives; he desires to fellowship with us, but he does not come uninvited. As Richard Foster observes,

If certain chambers of our heart have never experienced God's healing touch, perhaps it is because we have not welcomed the divine scrutiny. The most important work, most real, most lasting works is accomplished in the depths of our heart. The work is solitary and interior. It cannot be seen by anyone, not even ourselves. It is a work known only to God. It is the work of heart purity, of soul conversion, of inward transformation, of life formation.[10]

Even though we cannot see the work, it must be experienced by us in change that others will note. And that none of God's secret work will take place unless we take our place in submission before him. There is great mystery in all this. Just submit your spirit and start asking God, *Change my heart, shape my spirit, do your work.*

Reflections

King David was reported to be a man after God's own heart. This must have been because David's heart was trained to yearn for God. There is every reason from his actions to conclude that he was dedicated to God. David was a flawed man, but this does not preclude a strong heart and passion for God. David had "the sincere intention" of pleasing God. My evidence is Israel's songbook, the Psalter. David wrote the majority of the Psalms. One can't read them without experiencing the heights of their glory and the depths of their sorrow. One moment David sears with anger, the next he ascends to the heights of pleasure and devotion. And he usually ends in simple softness of heart and a vulnerable position of examination and submission to God. The Psalms speak for us, give words to our deepest urges, passions, and pain. So it is a strong heart for God, governed by the Holy Spirit, that will help us find the most honest and pleasant place in relationship to God.

CHAPTER 11

Uncomplicated Obedience

Is obedience to God ever easy? Can we get to a point where we want to obey more than disobey? Some believe so. There is a line of thought that champions the easy nature of living for Christ. Richard Foster writes, "Virtue is easy. . . . When the heart is purified by the action of the Spirit, the most natural thing in the world is the virtuous thing. To the pure in heart, vice is what is hard."[1] So the easy behavior comes as a result of a transformed nature; it is the product of the ancient practices called the spiritual disciplines.

Is this true? Is it possible for me to get to the place where I am able to walk past the pastry counter and feel nothing? To get to the place where I can stand in front of a pastry counter and picture a glazed doughnut as a dog bone or a bit of rubbish? After some spiritual training, will I want only what is good? Will I reach for the tray of carrots instead of the pastry?

Here is what I think is possible: Part of me will never stop wanting the doughnut, but given enough time and training, a better part of me will cause me to desire the better thing, in this case the tray of cold, crunchy carrots (see Galatians 5:16-17). The difference would be that I might taste the Lord and his ways and find them more delicious than anything else in life (see Psalm 34:8). So there is hope that I can make that transition. For if the Lord can't taste better than a carrot, then I have a problem, because carrots don't have a chance against doughnuts.

To Love Is to Obey

Dallas Willard advocates that through spiritual exercise, we can become the kind of people who naturally and easily do the things Jesus did—that we can think, act, and feel the way he did.[2] As we saw in the last chapter, William Law also believed that obedience is uncomplicated for those who sincerely want to please God. It's not that life suddenly becomes easy or that the development of the spiritual heart protects Christians from temptation and difficult or even horrific circumstances. There is an abundance of evidence, however, that saints past and present have found it painful, even agonizing, to disobey what they knew to be right. These words Martin Luther reportedly uttered have echoed over the centuries: "Here I stand, I can do no other." Luther could do only God's will; the agony of disobedience was too much to bear.

What I am saying is this: It is more difficult for a devoted follower of Christ to sin than to obey. By "devoted follower," I mean someone with relational closeness to Christ, for *devoted* means more than status with God. Relational closeness comes from investing time in submission to the practices that nurture the relationship: being with God, spending time in his Word, and hearing his voice.

Sadly, many Christians, while safely in the arms of God, are relationally distant from him. According to their theology of grace, which is passive, God does everything. Christians who believe they have no important role to play in purifying their hearts, who don't believe they need to be active participants, are believers filled with noble yet unfulfilled dreams.

It's clear that what Foster, Willard, and Law advocate as "easy" or "uncomplicated" is the result of discipline, practice, and a battle in the inner person over a sufficient period of time to train or transform the heart. I believe this is a lofty goal for all of us. I find it a bit idyllic because even the pure of heart find obedience hard and complex. Even more harshly, I don't find the idea of easy obedience in Scripture. Obedience didn't seem to get easy or uncomplicated for Paul.[3] *Uncomplicated*, then, means that our minds and hearts are in alignment with each other; even though we reach a maturity level, a level where Jesus dominates, we still experience an inner struggle.

Dallas Willard wrote, "Obedience is the only sound objective of a Christian spirituality."[4] Any Christian spirituality that does not lead to obedience is our enemy. Bonhoeffer agreed, saying that such theories should have a stake driven through their heart; they should be killed before they kill the church. Faith is real only in obedience; if faith is only pondering doing what God said, it is not faith. It may be a highly nuanced philosophy that animates the minds of those looking for reasons not to bow the knee to God. Such "faith" is useless, something to be thrown in the trash bin. If the end of a theory of spiritual formation does not lead to obedience, then that theory is delusionary because it teaches that obedience is optional.

We have learned thus far that what really matters is what we are like on the inside; that is where discipleship takes hold and where the foundation for obedience is laid. Jesus made obedience uncomplicated:

I have loved you even as the Father has loved me. Remain in my love. When you obey my commandments, you remain in my love, just as I obey my Father's commandments and remain in his love. (John 15:9-10)

Those who accept my commandments and obey them are the ones who love me. And because they love me, my Father will love them. And I will love them and reveal myself to each of them. (14:21)

In other words, if you love God, you will obey him. In that sense obedience is uncomplicated. Jesus modeled this for us in the way he related to his Father. Because he loved his Father, he desired to please him.[5] He poured out his heart to his Father from Gethsemane and the

Place of the Skull, saying, "My Father, if it is possible, may this cup be taken from me. Yet not as I will, but as you will" (Matthew 26:39, NIV). By his example, he is teaching us that when we love someone, we desire to please and do things that benefit the one we love even when we don't naturally want to do those things. We will unselfishly put that person's needs and desires above our own. Obedience is uncomplicated when someone who has given his or her life for you asks for your help. Your first impulse is to say yes. We know that "God loved the world so much that he gave his one and only Son, so that everyone who believes in him will not perish but have eternal life" (John 3:16). God spoke, God acted. Now what is my response? I respond with my life, with my obedience. I don't hesitate. Seen in this light, obedience is not complicated.

Why, then, do so many find obedience difficult?

The Complicated Heart

We all know that spiritual conflict lives in us all the days of our earthly life (see Galatians 5:17-26). What John Wesley and William Law meant by "perfect" is not what we mean today. When we say perfect, we refer to something that is unattainable. They meant maturity and made allowances for what they called ignorance and weakness. They believed that a person making progress toward Christlikeness would do so with a heart fully intent on pleasing God. Spiritual warfare is present in a person of vibrant faith, but that is different than a complicated heart.

James describes it for us:

> If you need wisdom, ask our generous God, and he will give it to you. He will not rebuke you for asking. But when you ask him, be sure that your faith is in God alone. Do not waver, for a person with divided loyalty is as unsettled as a wave of the sea that is blown and tossed by the wind. Such people should not expect to receive anything from the Lord. Their loyalty is

divided between God and the world, and they are unstable in everything they do. (1:5-8)

The complicated heart has divided loyalties; it has not made a decision with full intention. Your heart is "complicated" when you can't decide if you should marry a certain person or whether to buy a car or to take a new job. The complicated heart wobbles around. People with complicated hearts are unstable. One day they love, the next day they hate. The Christian with the complicated heart can't seem to get anywhere with God because he or she wants the benefits of faith and trust without faith and trust. It's the age-old problem of wanting to maintain control.

In my view, one reason for double-mindedness among thinking disciples is the whittling away of core Christian truth. The pressure on those who cling to orthodoxy is immense. The force of argument for tolerance is that of a tidal wave. Tolerance once meant that people would respect differences without accusation or name-calling. A Christian and Jew could disagree about the Messiah but respect each other's theological differences and care for each other. This is no longer the case. More and more people believe that to disagree is to disrespect.

A few days ago, a very well-meaning young man stood on my front porch and asked me for a donation to help get hate crime legislation written in the remaining twenty-two states where it does not exist. He said that the biggest haters in America were the evangelical Christians. He viewed himself as a carrier of love and Christians as purveyors of hate. It led to an interesting discussion.

Our current culture savagely attacks the ancient Christian doctrine that Jesus is the only way to salvation. Evangelicals are abandoning the exclusivity of the Christian message in droves; such things as the reality of hell, the absolutist claims of Scripture to be the Word of God, and so on are being discarded or shoved to the rear shelf, out of sight so as not to offend. Even well-meaning Christians, brave souls that go on talk shows, seem to soft peddle the not-so-good news to those who disagree. The few Christians who remain strong and say the truth are immediately assigned a label: bigot, hater, dinosaur, or Neanderthal.

This has weakened the level of conviction on the part of Christians in general, not only on the subjects already mentioned, but also on the very nature of God. Does he really care about the details of our lives? If not, whether because he doesn't care or he can't, then why pray? The common sentiment now is to look for the larger historical narrative, the meta-narrative that rises above conventional truth—not the kind you can verify but something beyond the limits of human reason and logic.

This theology has had a direct impact on the battle to obey. Fewer core Christian truths leads to fewer reasons to trust, pray, and obey. This has led to confused, less-confident Christians hesitant to invite God into their daily lives. They reason, *God can't be interested in my little problems given the hunger, war, and poverty in the world.* Another facet to this double-mindedness is the feeling of selfishness that comes upon those infected with this malaise. *It's petty and selfish of me to pray about my bad back when I have friends with cancer, job loss, and many disabilities.* This is exactly the way the Enemy wants to confuse us. He wants to create a God in our minds who is disgusted with our pettiness, self-indulgence, and weak spiritual constitutions.

The solution is not to abandon the search for truth or to stop wrestling with the hard and mystical. The solution is to know one's limits, to stop white-knuckling it through life by hanging on to control of our lives. The solution is to release control of our lives to God, to submit in obedience to him. Jesus told those who believed in him, "You are truly my disciples if you remain faithful to my teachings. And you will know the truth, and the truth will set you free" (John 8:31-32).

The truths that comfort are embraceable; you get at them with your heart and arms. They are too big for our minds. God makes sure our minds are involved, but it takes a whole person to embrace the whole God. This simplicity is indeed found on the other side of complexity. "If you try to hang on to your life, you will lose it. But if you give up your life for my sake, you will save it" (Luke 9:24).

Reflections

I love the poetry of William Blake. He was an engraver and one of the great Romantic poets of the late eighteenth and early nineteenth centuries. He was a man of faith, a mystic, and a bit strange according to his friends. On his deathbed, he burst out singing, laughing, and clapping his hands. He thought of death as simply moving from one room to another room, a simple transfer of being from this state to the next.

He lived in a culture that had been influenced by Voltaire and Rousseau. Voltaire, an Enlightenment scholar and a deist, said, if God did not exist, it would be necessary to invent him. Rousseau was much more a skeptic of religion than Voltaire. His writings were the foundation for the French Revolution, which for a time turned the great church Notre Dame into the Temple of Reason. Both men died in 1778 and are entombed in the Pantheon in Paris. For Blake, the men represented those who complicated faith, who allowed their great learning to create a deep skepticism about God.

The upcoming poem is Blake's call to reject the limited reason of humankind, because inevitably God wins. Blake, like many of us who follow Christ, knew that when you submit to God, everything about the world makes a lot more sense. There is now a resurgence of skepticism. The Voltaires and Rousseaus of our day are Christopher Hitchens, Sam Harris, and Richard Dawkins. They all are engaged in debate with evangelical scholars across America. The percentage of people who claim to be agnostic or atheist has grown a full 10 percent in the past decade. The American culture continues to accumulate reasons not to believe as a child. But anyone who has learned to follow Jesus knows the joy of trust. Trust continues to be the basis of a simplicity that makes life fit together the way the Creator designed it.

Mock on, Mock on Voltaire, Rousseau;
Mock on, Mock on: 'tis all in vain!

You throw the sand against the wind,
And the wind blows it back again.[6]

CHAPTER 12

Sustained Effort

No one is transformed by wishing it could happen. It is a choice. It takes place only when a disciple engages in a sustained effort. But this is difficult for some Christians to accept. One of the oddities of life is how much people revere hard work and how much Christians try to come to terms with it. Outside the religious realm, most believers are very hardworking. The Bible tells us to do everything with all our might. Whether it be loving God or working at a bakery, don't hold back (see 1 Corinthians 10:31; Colossians 3:23). But when talk about working hard to develop a heart for God comes up, many immediately recoil, saying, "Oh, we don't do it! God does it all!"

There is this gulf between the real world, where hard work is universally praised, and the religious world, where many are still trying to calibrate its role. This problem has to do with the confusion over the nature of grace—not only about what grace is but also about what it does and how it relates to human effort. Grace is what we call the act of God whereby he captures our hearts, implants new life in us, and gives us the desire to serve him and, through the Holy Spirit, the power to do it. God delivers his grace to the world through humans, and the delivery system is the body. That is why Paul told us to present our bodies as living sacrifices (see Romans 12:1). A completely animated body employs its full power in mind, soul, strength, and heart (see mark 12:30). I'm reminded of Olympic athlete Eric Liddell's well-known line from the film *Chariots of Fire*, "God made me fast, and when I run, I feel his pleasure." This is the high point for all human beings in the service of God: to take what God has made them and give a full effort. There is great joy in this.

Effort is good; the Scriptures extol its benefits.[1] Many Christians would say, "Grace is not opposed to effort; it is opposed to earning. God's grace is a gift and is not for sale or given to the hardest worker." However, grace endows one with the power and resources to give a full effort (see Ephesians 2:8-10). Paul's autobiographical teaching gives credence to the mystical relationship of grace and effort:

> We tell others about Christ, warning everyone and teaching everyone with all the wisdom God has given us. We want to present them to God, perfect in their relationship to Christ. That's why I work and struggle so hard, depending on Christ's mighty power that works within me. (Colossians 1:28-29)

Paul worked hard; he struggled, but it is with God's power that he did so. That is the divine dance we do every day. We join hands with Jesus; he leads and we follow.

Choosing to Take Action

When we choose to take action, employing the tools God has given us, we are demonstrating our "full intention" to please God, which is what creates an uncomplicated spiritual heart. These tools are commonly known as spiritual disciplines. Their usefulness in forming Christ in us is essential.

Many have employed these tools without ever hearing the term *spiritual disciplines*. It's also true that a person with a heart for God will do them and not even think of them as disciplines. Some people enjoy doing hard things. For example, it is hard work to train for the Olympic decathlon, which involves ten track and field events that take place over a two-day period. The training requires years of hard work, but decathletes get joy and satisfaction in their training. If they didn't, they would never last. What starts out as hard doesn't remain hard when joy enters the process. Just try to keep a person away from a demanding chore if he or she loves it. The person with a heart for God feels the same way about the spiritual disciplines.

For the record, the spiritual disciplines are normally understood to be the following: Bible reading, meditating on Scripture, memorization, prayer, silence, solitude, worship, evangelism, service, stewardship, fasting, silence, solitude, submission, and frugality.[2] These disciplines are the exercises of Christian training and enable us to be with God, read his Word, and hear his voice. They are to the Christian what training is to a long-distance runner. When the runner leaves the ceremony and cheers of the starting line, all she can hear is rhythmic breathing and the pounding of feet. At first, the training can feel like drudgery. But if she sticks with it day after day, eventually the sounds, the feel of the air, and the rising strength in her body become addictive. She has to run. But it all started with weaker lungs and sore legs, with only a desire to become something she wasn't. Spiritual training works the same way. The spiritual heart can be trained by employing these God-given tools. We start with desire to be like Christ, and through sustained effort and God's power, we become Christlike.

Why the Critics Are Wrong

It is critical at this point to say that the only reason we have to practice the disciplines is that Jesus practiced them. Critics of the spiritual disciplines claim they are a product of medieval monasticism,[3] that they are Catholic in origin and should be avoided. They go on to point out that they are not listed in Scripture, nor does Scripture tell us to practice them. What the critics miss is that the disciplines are embedded in Jesus' life. He prayed alone, fasted, spent extended time alone, and lived a life of frugality. His life was a model of service, submission, sacrifice, and evangelism. It is obvious that he understood Scripture and had memorized much of it.[4]

It should also be noted that Jesus didn't practice these disciplines in a legalistic way. He was not uptight about them; they flowed out of his natural life. They are the things he did based on his nature. *Healthy* and *balanced* are the operative words. Did Jesus mature and grow as a person because of them? Was their practice a natural expression of who he was? To answer these questions, we would need to revisit the arguments of several church councils. I will resist that temptation and venture to say that the answer to both questions is yes. The mystery of the God-man teaches us that Jesus grew as a human being. He had to learn to read, he had to apprentice under his father to learn the skills of a carpenter, so it seems clear that he did benefit from study, prayer, and meditation on Scripture as he grew into adulthood. At the same time, he was unable to sin. He was tempted like us and to a much higher degree, but he escaped without sin. Because we are imperfect, and that is an understatement, we fail regularly. The practice of spiritual disciplines in my life is irregular, shot through with inconsistency, and my motives are a twisted mystery. But I do them because Jesus practiced them.

So did the early Christians. They were taught to cross the road to help someone in distress and to help the least of humans. When they loved the difficult and carried other people's burdens, they didn't identify it as, "I am practicing the disciplines." When they gathered for worship, submitted to their leaders, fasted, and collected money for hungry Christians, they didn't say, "I am in a training program." But they were exhorted to love, to help, to pray, to be in submission to authority, and to follow the example of their leaders. They were famous for taking care of one another and for nursing the sick during plagues. All the spiritual disciplines were there, exercised through the disciplined will of a community committed to behaving as Jesus would if he were in their place.

The Power of the Disciplines

Dallas Willard speaks to the power of these practices. "The spiritual disciplines are essential to the deliverance of human beings from the concrete power of sin."[5] By "the concrete power of sin," he means actual habits that are the footings for sin. Sin is more than a theory, something to be batted around by philosophers and theologians. It often manifests itself in real actions that harm and hurt. It takes more than forgiveness of those sins to change us. The forgiveness of sin is essential to fellowship with God, to a new relationship with him, but it does not help us deal with sin on a practical level. For that we need to practice the disciplines, so the heart can be transformed. For instance, the sin of prayerlessness is set in the concrete habit of not making time to meet with God. The solution begins with the concrete habit of making that time through the practice of the spiritual disciplines. Setting aside time to hear from God and to reflect on his Word does not change a person; it only positions a person to change. Commitment to the practice of these disciplines also says something about the person's desire to change; therefore, they are tools God uses. Something now is possible that was not when that person was not setting aside time to hear from God. The objective for practicing the spiritual disciplines is to have Christ formed in us; therefore, we rearrange our practices around his practices.

If we choose to practice the disciplines, God puts the desire in our heart to be like him. If we do practice them, they then become a habit, which affects our character, and the result is a transformed heart, an uncomplicated spiritual heart. Let me explain.

Faith Is Action

When new life is resident in a person, it gives that person both the desire and intention to be like Christ. Second Corinthians 5:15-17 says,

He died for everyone so that those who receive his new life will no longer live for themselves. Instead, they will live for Christ, who died and was raised for them.

So we have stopped evaluating others from a human point of view. At one time we thought of Christ merely from a human point of view. How differently we know him now! This means that anyone who belongs to Christ has become a new person. The old life is gone; a new life has begun!

Change begins with the regenerate heart, for only the regenerate heart has the capacity for transformation into Christlikeness. This is why I have insisted that Christian spiritual formation is unique. Part of us yearns for a closer relationship with God.[6] That is the basis for any act of faith, or, as I like to call it, action. Desire and intention are proved real only when there is action. Bonhoeffer was fond of saying, "Only the obedient believe and only those who believe are obedient . . . that faith is only real in obedience."[7] Faith is not faith unless it acts (see James 2:14-16). Jesus said that faith was following him and answering the call to ministry (see Luke 9:23-27). If a person has a desire to be kind to a difficult person, then faith is taking specific actions of kindness toward that person.

Sadly, the faith of the Western church has been reduced to intellectual agreement and has been divorced from action. Not to say that Christians in the West haven't taken a great deal of action. It is just that they call it service or missions, but they don't equate it with faith as the word is used in reference to salvation. That kind of faith does not transform the heart because it is not faith at all. A person's immaterial nature or spiritual heart is transformed by acting in faith on its desire to please God. This is the beginning, and one right act can make a difference in a person's life and for those touched by their action. A single act of forgiveness can restore a life; a generous gift can turn a life around. But there is more to be done in order for these good actions to be turned into one's character and to develop an uncomplicated spiritual heart.

Habits Become Our Character

The continued actions of faith based on desire or intention eventually transform the heart. Such sustained effort requires discipline, which most of us do not have. The good news, however, is that God knows this and has a solution. His solution is that we practice these disciplines in community, in relationship to others of kindred spirit and intent. When Paul exhorted Timothy, "Discipline yourself for the purpose of godliness" (1 Timothy 4:7, NASB), he was not advocating a singular effort but one joined to the community. One of the joys of life together in Christ is to help one another keep our commitments to God. Everyone knows how hard it is to break bad habits and make new ones. That is the reason God has given us the gift of spiritual friends, friends who will love and support us. Only humble people will submit themselves to others and allow their character to be developed in community. One of the many reasons God is opposed to the proud is that pride blocks one's growth and transformation (see 1 Peter 5:5-6). People who live in a spiritual community with helpful relationships and who jointly practice the spiritual disciplines discover their hearts being transformed. Their hearts for God grow stronger and more passionate. And undergirding the whole process is the proactive effort of practicing the disciplines that God says will help us.

The Spiritual Heart Manages Character

The end result is a nonconflicted spiritual heart that has a passionate intent to serve God and is trained to do so. One of the most helpful distinctions in the use of words is the one between *trying* and *training*. The life of transformation takes time, and the word *trying* communicates effort that is in a hurry. It has a deadline rather than a goal. *Training*, however, indicates process, and it leaves room for patience. It gives our lives the space for unexpected events, setbacks, mistakes, and, let's face it, stupidity. Like an athlete preparing for a major event that is months or years away, we need to take the long view because the spiritual life is a journey. All the while, the spiritual heart directs the effort with passion and discipline.

Reflections

The sustaining of effort requires a vision, and that is found primarily in living in a healthy spiritual community. It's easier to keep the vision in our sights when others can remind us of what it is. The discipline required to sustain the work of spiritual growth comes not so much from each individual as from the collective will of the community. In the next chapter, we'll look more closely at how this works.

CHAPTER 13

Structure and Accountability in Community

Dietrich Bonhoeffer understood how much Christians need each other. Who among us can deny the penetrating truthfulness of his words below?

> God has willed that we should seek and find his living Word in the witness of a brother, in the mouth of a man. Therefore, the Christian needs another Christian who speaks God's Word to him. He needs him again and again when he becomes uncertain and discouraged, for by himself he cannot help himself without belying the truth the Christ in his own heart is weaker than the Christ in the word of his brother; his own heart is uncertain, his brother's is sure.[1]

Christians should never take it for granted that we are privileged to live among other Christians, for God chooses to use other believers to keep us going. When we become uncertain and weak, it is another Christ follower who is not confused, who is certain, and who strengthens us with God's Word in that moment.

The Problem with Church People

There is much to commend itself for staying away from church people. The stigma now being attached to Christians for holding their religious convictions is enough to keep the fearful away. Who wants to be a member of a hate group, as some would accuse? There is a new play that has opened on the Internet called *Proposition Hate*.[2] Several big-name stars are in the production, which portrays those who oppose gay marriage as bigots and hate mongers. This does not create any negative press for those hating the "haters." No one seems to wonder, *Isn't that just as intolerant and hateful to treat people of faith the way we accuse them of treating the gay marriage issue?* For all the talk about free speech, freedom of expression, and tolerance, there is no fascism like liberal, happy-face fascism.

It will increasingly become more risky to hold any serious opinion that disagrees with popular culture. In such a world, as Bonhoeffer says, "words lose their weight." All serious questions fall prey to the incredible lightness of being. When Bonhoeffer was negotiating the subject of his speech at the 1934 Fano conference that would decide if German Christian leaders would choose to support national socialism or break with the prevailing winds, he wrote, "Only truth and complete truthfulness can help us now."[3] Bonhoeffer's commitment to truth would never be tolerated in today's philosophical climate. The man whom the political left loves to lionize would be labeled a bigot, much like the Nazis he fought and who in the end executed him. Heinrich Himmler signed Bonhoeffer's death warrant; today it would be *The New York Times*.

Then there is the problem of the church telling the truth about our lives. I don't think this is a problem in the creedal sense. We freely admit that we are sinners in need of a Savior and that confession of sin and forgiveness and reconciliation are daily essentials. The dishonesty is evident in the smallest ways. Many Christians never admit to watching television or attending movies. The rule is, never admit any connection to popular culture. Never say you love Larry David's *Curb Your Enthusiasm* or *Saturday Night Live* or know Madonna's tour schedule. Anything most church members know about sin, they learned by accident. There is little truth-telling in the church about our pathologies of materialism, sexual repression, and exhibitionism or about how precarious our commitments to Christ actually are. If there is anything we know for sure, it's that the church isn't hip, and when it tries, it makes many laugh out loud. I recently saw a pastor on television making crème brûlée. He was working from a full kitchen set like you would see on the Food Network. Every week he makes something different and uses it as a way to explain Christian living. Is this wrong? No, but it so trivialized the points he was making I was laughing out loud. (He was cooking pasta and trying to explain the Trinity by saying that the pasta was the Father, the meatballs Jesus, and the red sauce the Holy Spirit.) So if you want to be relevant, stay away from churches.

The Human Condition

But despite the many reasons for staying away from it, the church has a grip on me. I can't live with it and I can't live without it. My distain for the shortcomings and sins of other believers is a reflection of my unmet need to feel superior or different from them. I desperately need other Christians to rescue me from my own self-importance. Bonhoeffer put it well when he said, "One who wants fellowship without solitude plunges into the void of words and feelings, and one who seeks solitude without fellowship perishes in the abyss of vanity, self-infatuation and despair."[4] Keeping other Christians at arm's length is a way to seek the benefits of fellowship without the cost, but true fellowship will cost you your life.

I've lost count of how many times I've been discouraged about my ministry. In those moments of weakness, God always sent someone to speak his word of encouragement to me: "Be steadfast, immovable, always abounding in the work of the Lord, knowing that in the Lord your labor is not in vain" (1 Corinthians 15:58, RSV). Other times I've been wrong about something, and God sent someone to save me from my own self-destruction. (I'll give you a specific example of this later.) Then there was the case of my oldest son.

One day I got a call that my son had been caught smoking pot at school and I was to come collect him. When I arrived, I was met by the high school principal and a police officer. They told me that they had decided not to arrest my son but to instead expel him from the school. He would be transferred to the other high school in the area. When I made eye contact with my son, I was wondering, *Who is this boy?* We drove away in silence, neither of us knowing what to say. I didn't know what to do. Should I resign from the church? After all, my son was rebellious. What should I do? That night I had forty men at my house to watch the NCAA basketball finals. I was there, but not really. I smiled, I conversed, but it all seemed like a dream.

The next few years were tumultuous. It was the Christians in our lives who got us through it and brought it all to a good end. I felt I should resign, but the elders helped me separate out my fathering efforts from my son's bad choices. The congregation got behind our family financially. Individuals approached us and asked to help pay the expenses that our son's care required. For more than three years, people from various churches made monthly contributions that paid all the expenses. Not one person left the church over this family problem, and no one ever brought up my son's difficulties in order to be critical of me. Everyone realized the great deal of pain our family was in, and they supported us through it all. I have served in environments of shame and accusation; they are common in churches. I thank God that I was not in a negative environment at that time, where hiding sin, covering up, and pretending that Christians don't have problems is the norm.

The Value of Structure and Accountability

What I have described is structure and accountability clothed in love and relationships. There is no better place to find this than the local church, where Christians gather on a regular basis to be encouraged to go back into society and be "little Christs" who change what they touch.

When you want to grow spiritually, you need several things working for you. You need the desire to grow and change, submission to a plan or person, and a commitment to practice daily. Then you form a habit, and that habit of kindnesses, gentleness, returning good for evil, reading the Scriptures, or conversing with God through prayer forms your character. Just as in almost every area of live, when you practice and form a new habit, it changes you. I know this; I feel much better after I pray and meditate on Scripture than when I skip it. You can't get where you want to go without structure. It empowers, it will lift you out of failure, and it is God's way for a more blessed life.

I have heard it said by people I respect that you can't program transformation; it is too organic and authentic to be organized. When the yearning for no programs becomes a philosophical position, the word *naïve* is appropriate. This position is based on the loftiest of goals, that much prayer and meditation will replace the need for study guides and meetings. I would agree that structures that don't enlist people in spiritual exercises are sure to fail in that they allow people to stay fixed where they are. Very few among us are hungry or desperate enough to break out of nonproductive patterns. Without some kind of structure, most of us will naturally stagnate. Living in a society saturated in noise means that we don't take the time to listen to our spiritual impulses. The more we have materially, the less likely it is that we will have to face ourselves.

Frankly, most of us require pain to consider changing our behavior and attitudes. For example, preventative health care is a tough sell; it asks you to submit yourself to some unseemly medical procedures. On top of that, you are exhorted to exercise regularly and eat right. Although people will admit that it is right, saying, "I should do those things, but I never seem to get around to it," only about 30 percent of the population takes up any of this good advice. Many Christians respond the same when asked to exercise spiritually, to be disciplined with a good spiritual diet. If it doesn't hurt, then why change? Most of us don't think about the disease and trouble we avoid by taking preventive measures. Empirical data on the health benefits of not eating brownies is not yet available; the exquisite joy of a warm brownie in one's mouth while listening to "Silent Night" is.

Needed: A Spiritual Training Program

Life itself is a tougher obstacle course than any of us would design for ourselves. But if we want to be able to react to and endure the challenges of life, wouldn't it make sense to train so we can do what needs to be done when it needs to be done? The words of Saint Paul come to mind:

> Don't you realize that in a race everyone runs, but only one person gets the prize? So run to win! All athletes are disciplined in their training. They do it to win a prize that will fade away, but we do it for an eternal prize. So I run with purpose in every step. I am not just shadowboxing. *I discipline my body like an athlete, training it to do what it should.* Otherwise, I fear that after preaching to others I myself might be disqualified. (1 Corinthians 9:24-27, emphasis added)

Paul had a healthy fear of not performing at the highest level. Some might consider it a "hangover" from his days as a Pharisee, where the striving for performance was pathological. But I wonder if it might be the healthy yearning of a man who had been in God's presence more than once. Perhaps Paul had it more right than those who never fear that their lives won't be a maximum offering to Christ, for whom grace is an excuse for a feeble effort. He said, "I discipline my body like an athlete, training it to do what it should." Paul thought of his body as his servant, as something trained to do what it should. He didn't think of his body as his master, like those who are enslaved to the body's appetites and limitations.

What do athletes do when they train? They employ a coach, join a club, or submit themselves to a coach through a school. Coaches are essential because we are not as objective about our abilities and needs as a skilled coach is. Good coaches tell the truth and help athletes work on areas of weakness. They push athletes beyond what they believe they can do and hold them accountable when it comes to sticking with the training program. A coach also designs an exercise program that includes what their athletes need to do and why and how often they need to do it and when.

Many years ago, I was on a traveling basketball team. We were touring South America, playing twenty games in twenty-eight days. It was a grueling regime. We would stay up late every night attending receptions or playing games. We would typically get to bed around two in the morning and arise in a few hours to travel to the next destination. I vividly recall one weekend we had a day off; we were thrilled not to have to play or practice because there was no practice facility available, but our coach decided we would run up and down the stairwells of the hotel for thirty minutes in order to stay sharp. We were incredulous that he would push us that hard for no reason we could imagine. The lesson missing on us that day was that we easily were able to run up and down stairwells for thirty minutes; we were in superb condition.

A good coach calls you and gets you out there when you don't feel like it. But as a result, something begins to happen: You slowly form a habit. Once the habit is formed, it becomes part of you. You have to exercise; your body hurts when you don't work out. So you start looking at your watch, trying to figure out how you might find time to don those togs. You start planning your week; if there are meetings that conflict with your exercise schedule, you write, "Get up at 5:30, exercise."

Some of you are thinking, *That could never happen to me.* That may be true when it comes to physical exercise, but it can be you and spiritual exercise. After all, this began with a Pauline metaphor. Once again the words Paul used were "training it to do what it should." He was talking about bringing all of our personhood and personality into submission to Christ and his plan for our lives. If we don't have a coach to hold us accountable, we won't succeed at doing this. How many more times do we need to fail to prove the truth of this simple idea?

The Church as the Coach

Our coach can be a person, a program, or a group of like-minded people. Most often it is a small group sponsored by a church or Christian organization. The Willow Creek Community Church's Reveal study surveyed eighty thousand members of more than five hundred churches. It found that the primary reason people reengaged spiritually was because their church leaders encouraged it and that people reengaged through personal spiritual practices, which were: (1) prayer to seek guidance, (2) prayer to confess sins, (3) Bible reading, (4) reflection on Scripture, and (5) solitude. The study revealed that other factors for waking people up spiritually—such as personal crisis, inspiration, life change, switching churches, serving experiences, and counseling—all finished far behind. The study also found that the spiritually mature do these five activities less than 60 percent of the time.[5] This demonstrates that, at least among mainstream white Christians, no one is perfectly consistent in spiritual practices, supporting my point that successful spiritual growth is not for the loner; it is for those who humbly cluster together and lean on one another. The cherry on top is the study's general conclusion: "The Church is the most significant organized influence on spiritual growth, so the activities of the church naturally emerge as important catalytic factors."[6] I suppose the best advice for Christians—whether young, old, mature, struggling, or estranged—remains "Go to church."

And once you are there, latch on to those who are doing the spiritual practices. You might approach people who seem to have the qualities you admire and meet with them. Interview them about their lives and ask them about the people and events that formed them. Spending time with fellow followers of Christ who are kindred spirits will be vital to your growth. Over a lifetime, you will need several different kinds of people to walk with you; there are different seasons, different challenges, but they are all to be found among fellow Christ followers.

What are you committing to when you join a church? The common assumption is that you will attend weekend services regularly and contribute some money to help support the staff and programs of the church. You might join a group or take a special seminar, but beyond that, the pastor has no further claim on you. If this is your understanding, joining a church will fail to have any substantial effect on your spiritual growth. What is needed is a deep enough trust to submit to the leadership of the church and the direction of the Holy Spirit. Only then will there be progress. That is when you submit to training.

Training Your Entire Person to Do What It Should

Throughout this book, we've discussed the spiritual exercises that make up this training. Training involves reading, memorizing, meditating, and praying through the Scriptures. It also means periodically getting alone with God for times of solitude and reflection and loosening our grip on our selfishness through giving, serving, frugality, and fasting. Add to this the exercise of spiritual gifts in the service of others, such as mercy, helps, and teaching, exhorting, and so on.

In the best of church worlds, the pastor teaches the value of discipleship and spiritual exercise. Then the group life of the church is organized around these practices so that people can grow together in Christlikeness. People can't become Christlike without accountability, and they can't have accountability without structure, but that structure can be as simple as "We will meet every Tuesday morning at eight and discuss chapter 8 of our book on the spiritual disciplines."

The Necessary Ingredients for Spiritual Growth

Most decisions for Christ are not a conversion; they are about entering into a community of Christ followers and submitting to their rule of life. "By now dozens of close-up studies of conversion have been conducted. All of them confirm that social networks are the basic mechanism through which conversion takes place."[7] As Lesslie Newbigin has said, "The greatest hermeneutic of the gospel is a community that seeks to live by it."[8] The qualities necessary for spiritual growth are to be found in any community—a family, a church or small group, a business or organization, a team. The community could be as small as two people or as big as thousands of people. But once a community contains more than twenty people, it needs to break down into smaller groups in order to retain these qualities. As Newbigin says, the gospel needs to be practiced, not just believed. In order to flourish, people need to be part of a community that has the qualities of trust, grace, humility, submission, and affirmation. Let's take a look at each.

Trust

This is the most important requirement for spiritual development: finding at least one person in your community that you can trust. Trust is based on integrity; you can trust a person who has proven to be reliable and honest. However, this doesn't mean that person always agrees with your ideas or supports your behavior. It means you can trust him or her to listen to you without judging or condemning you when you ask for help to overcome a persistent sin in your life. When you find someone you can trust, then you can be vulnerable with that person. You can allow yourself to come under that person's influence. Trust is key, because you will take in only the truth you trust, and that trust has to do with the messenger as much as the message. When you become vulnerable with someone, you're giving that person permission to speak into your life.

Here's an example of what I mean. Recently I have been trying to figure out retirement. I have no plans to retire, but age slows us down and eventually we have no choice but to work less. I have a close friend with whom I meet regularly who has contributed a great deal to my life. I trust him completely, so I opened up to him about my financial life, plans, dreams, fears, and indecision. I asked him, "Am I thinking straight?" I became vulnerable in that I chose to be influenced by him. At the same time, I didn't want to put him in a position of taking responsibility for my decision. That would be unhealthy.

Choose the person carefully because his or her character will help shape yours. Look for someone whose actions reflect his or her words, someone whose character you admire, someone with a reputation for confidentiality. If you can't find such a person, pray! Pray fervently. God will be faithful in giving you such a person. Above all, don't give up. Keep searching and praying. Relationships of trust provide the foundation for transformational discipleship. They enable us to deal honestly with the barriers to obedience and overwhelming sins that hold us back from spiritual growth. Certainly it requires courage to say to God, *Lord, I'm not afraid of you using*_____ (insert the person's name) *to make changes in my life*. The result of this vulnerability will reflect what Jesus described: When a student is fully taught, he "will become like the teacher" (Luke 6:40).

Grace

In order to grow in Christlikeness, you'll also need to be part of a community that offers you grace, particularly when you stumble and fall. To offer grace means treating others better than they deserve to be treated. It means looking past faults to give others our praise and support. Most of us have trouble offering grace on our own, but when we tap into God as our resource, we can draw on the grace he pours out onto every person. God treats us all much better than we deserve to be treated. When a community of Christians creates an environment of grace, the result is a culture of acceptance in which people see the value and good in others. This is true in our homes, in our neighborhoods, with spiritual friends, or in a church environment. This doesn't mean we ignore sins, faults, and problems. But when Christians offer people a place where they feel safe, affirmed, and able to risk, they'll be more open about their sins and weakness and more open to working on changing those things that hold them back spiritually. I believe this is why our house is full of visitors. Jane, my wife, is a person who attracts women who love to drop in and talk about their lives and struggles and have a cup of tea. It is an environment of grace that draws them.

When I mentioned the need for grace to a friend, he objected to the idea that we should overlook people's weaknesses and focus on their strengths. He claimed this would allow people to be sloppy. But that isn't what happens in an environment of grace. In such an environment, people feel safe and affirmed; they open up to others' input into their lives. Think about your own experiences. When someone who loves you speaks into your life and affirms what you do well, you welcome it. The people who love you and whom you trust have incredible power and influence over you.

When you can answer the question "Can I trust me with you?" with a resounding "Yes!" discipleship will work as you make yourself available for transformation. You will feel free to explore your options. You will be more willing to confess your sins and ask for forgiveness. You may be willing to write or paint, or sing, or attempt a new profession. An environment of grace frees you to be whom God says you are.

Humility

The process of transformation has two kinds of curriculum. The first is our planned experiences, small groups, seminars, and what the religious world creates. The second is the big curriculum, which is daily life. A community that will foster spiritual growth is one that will teach you how to humbly receive life as it comes hurling at you. Humility is simply the acknowledgment of who you are dependent on. When your answer is Christ, then you will have humility.

Pride blocks God's grace from our lives, homes, relationships, and churches. This book is about being formed in Christ and what a difference that can make in the world. One reason even the best discipleship plans don't result in transformation is they don't start with humility.

To be humble means to "make oneself low, to level a mountain, to bow down, or to be a person of the earth." Without humility, Christ wouldn't have submitted himself to the Father or made the sacrifice of his own life for the whole world. Humility, Christ's primary character trait, is square one for personal transformation. That is why we must engage in its development in our character. Humility forms the environment and relationships that make transformation possible.

Just as humility is Jesus' primary character trait, it should be the foundation you build on as you seek to follow him and be formed into his image: "Humble yourselves, therefore, under God's mighty hand, that he may lift you up in due time" (1 Peter 5:6, NIV). Think of it this way: Without humility, there's no submission; without submission, there are no relationships of trust; without relationships of trust, you won't make yourself vulnerable; unless you make yourself vulnerable, no one can influence you; and without the influence of others, you won't change.

Jesus' humility allowed him to divest himself of the rights and privileges of deity, enabling him to submit himself to the will and agenda of his Father.

Submission

In order to grow spiritually, you also need to be part of a community that encourages submission. *Submission* is a love word before it is an authority word.[9] We submit to others because we desire to enter into a relationship that benefits us and those around us. It doesn't involve someone "keeping us in line," but it allows someone to help us keep our commitments to God, to hold us accountable.

I would like to think that I don't need someone else to tell me what to do and then check and see if I did it, but without such a person or system, I would be a disaster. Here's a case in point. I once insisted on a raise, a big raise—I'm talking a 33 percent increase in salary. The church board offered me a hundred dollars a month; I was insulted and turned it down. Two of the board members, who were also longtime friends, asked me to meet with them. After a few niceties, one of them said, "Bill, it's time to grow up. We can't afford more than this and you need to take it." The other friend agreed. He even suggested that if I did a better job, I might get more pay. Ah, the wounds of a friend; they spoke God's truth to me. They pointed out that I was to be a servant, an example to the flock. That was my first and most important duty. I respected these men; I valued their advice because I knew them to be well-trained disciples. They knew the Scriptures; they shared their faith; they were faithful to serve; they could hear God's voice. This all goes back to their being men who had chosen the life of following Jesus. And they had done more than simply wish to be mature in Christ; they had gone on the journey of learning from Jesus how to live their lives. These are the kinds of people it is a privilege to submit to.

As I discovered, when we practice submission in community, three things happen: (1) our needs get met; (2) we get to practice humility, the character trait that allows us to submit; and (3) we allow others to love us. This makes us growing disciples who then influence others with our Christlikeness. Nothing could be more radical or counter-cultural than Christians who submit to other people's needs. This is a key place where churches and ministries should invest their energy. Living this way would send our paltry efforts to be relevant through new worship forms, hip looks, and trendy language to the ash heap of irrelevancy. Certainly efforts to renew and redefine worship and connect with cultural trends have their place, but they pale in the face of what will happen when the people of God submit to each other and live for each other.

Affirmation

Finally, spiritual growth is fostered in communities that promote affirmation. We all need affirmation. It confirms our identities. It lets us know that others appreciate our strengths and contributions, and this helps us risk coming out of our shells.

When others don't affirm us, we begin to affirm ourselves. If no one pays attention to us, we start doing things to get others to notice us. Obvious examples include the blowhard at a party or the teenager who acts up at school. Even if we don't go to that extent, most of us end up affirming ourselves at times. Think about it. Let's say you are sitting in a meeting at work for hours and no one notices you. When you finally speak up, your thoughts are dismissed. How do you feel? Do you get anxious and look for opportunities to score points to bolster your sinking feelings of insignificance? This scenario is sad for at least two reasons. First, if you knew that the group fully accepted and respected you, you could relax and be yourself. Second, the fact that we all relate to this scenario reveals our pathological dependence on others for our identity. Now let's paint a different scene. What if the meeting started with an exercise of affirmation to reinforce your gifts and communicate how others feel about your contribution? This would create a safe environment where you could relax and give genuine input.

Here's another example of affirmation: When Paul left his position as pastor of the church at Ephesus, Timothy was his successor. It's tough enough to follow a hardworking and gifted person, let alone an apostle! Timothy was younger, known to have a nervous tummy, shy, and easily intimidated (see 1 Timothy 4:11-16; 2 Timothy 1:7-8; 2:1; 4:1-4). Surely he heard lots of opinions about how he compared to Paul and how he should conduct his work as pastor. Paul, a passionate man who loved and hated with great force, sensed Timothy's needs and began his second letter to him with these powerful affirmations (see 2 Timothy 1:3-4):

I thank God for you.
I pray for you night and day.
I think about you all the time.
I remember your tears.
I long to see you.
I am filled with joy when I am around you.

Affirmation is powerful. It creates an environment that gives people permission to drop their defenses, and that allows deep change to take place. I've never known affirmation to arouse sin, and the belief that it does reveals a twisted theology. When I receive praise, I want to do better. When a brother or sister in the faith affirms me, I don't become conceited; instead, I feel humbled that God thinks so much of me that he sends one of his children to affirm me. The messenger is almost as good as a dove descending and a voice from heaven saying, "This is my beloved child in whom I am well pleased." For that reason, I want to make an even greater effort.

Affirmation becomes a way of life in an environment of grace. It reminds people that God values them. This is more than theology; it's a truth they experience. Affirmation allows people to be broken before God and to deal with unconfessed sin, shame, and the other inner-life issues that destroy our good effort at discipleship.

Questions Each Member Must Answer

Trust, grace, humility, submission, affirmation — these foundational and essential elements create community. Suspicion, criticism, pride, self-will, and competition — these caustic and damaging qualities destroy community. Every community includes all of these, so each member must decide the following:

- Will I endeavor to live as a person of trust, grace, humility, submission, and affirmation?
- Will I be an example of these traits of Christ to others so we can create the kind of community in which disciples can grow?
- Will I help my fellow disciples to be able to answer yes to the question "Can I trust me with you?"

The desired result is an agape love toward others. Agape love is a giving love. It is more than intention; it is action that is for the benefit of others. As I have said, we don't get there by wishing we had this kind of love; we get there through spiritual exercise. But it takes a community of Christians who can provide us with a structure that will hold us accountable and offer us the things we need in order to grow spiritually.

Reflections

Does being Christlike matter? Will it change anything? Skeptics report that the problem throughout history has been religion and religious people. They assert that much evil has been done in the name of God and claim that only when we can extract ourselves from such foolishness does the world have a chance of being a civil place. I believe that the answer is not the absence of religion but the proper application of it. Instead of thinking primarily of civil, social, or political change through religion, the revolution is internal. It is the transformation of persons from the inside out. The solution is a transformation of character, which will lead to individuals affecting their families, workplaces, societies, nations, and world. As we conclude this argument, we now turn our attention to how that change can take place. You won't be shocked if it involves being a special person that Jesus commanded us to make and has called every one of us to be.

CHAPTER 14

Can a Privatized Spirituality Change the World?

Jesus taught that what comes out of our heart either rewards or judges us and also reveals the content of our heart (see Luke 6:43-45). What is in people always comes out; it always affects those around them. What's inside their hearts can not remain hidden. It must come out in actions. Disciples who are truly alive in Christ are like a lit match; they will start a fire.

Most of us have a box of matches in the house. Grab a handful and lay them on a table. All you have are many matches doing nothing. If, however, you strike one, the rest of the pile ignites and you have fire. Jesus championed the idea that from one little light, a difference can be made:

> You are the light of the world—like a city on a hilltop that cannot be hidden. No one lights a lamp and then puts it under a basket. Instead, a lamp is placed on a stand, where it gives light to everyone in the house. In the same way, let your good deeds shine out for all to see, so that everyone will praise your heavenly Father. (Matthew 5:14-16)

This kind of passion begins on the inside, so some might say that only a privatized spirituality can change the world. Because belief or faith that doesn't spring from inside a person will flame out; it won't be real. True faith begins inside us, in the privacy of the heart, but it can not remain there; it must be displayed. By its nature the flame is ignited, and before you know it you have what Elton Trueblood called "incendiary fellowship."[1] It is by the faith of others that our faith is ignited, which is why there can never be churchless Christianity.

Faith that springs from inside us shines. It talks, it walks, it interacts, it cares. It is God's active presence in the world. "When Blasé Pascal needed language to express the vivid character of his life changing experience in November, 1654, he wrote in large letters, on his secret document, the word, FIRE."[2] He described his encounter with God as "Joy, joy, joy, and tears of joy."[3] After his death, the secret document was found sewn into the lining of his coat; the passion for Christ burned deep within him.

The reason Christians have trouble igniting passion in others is that we function as unlit matches, lying there with the potential for fire, but unstruck. There is an anonymous prayer that can act as an antidote:

Come as the fire and burn
Come as the wind and cleanse
Come as a light and reveal.
Convict, convert, consecrate
Until we are wholly thine.

However, not all Christian leaders and thinkers agree with this view.

Au Contraire

Sociologist James Davidson Hunter of the University of Virginia argues that it is not the inner conversion of the heart and mind that enables a person to have the right values and make the right choices. He suggests that this view has caused many to mistakenly believe that world change could come from evangelism. Hunter believes that the error of this perspective derives from three sources deep in modern Western thought. The first is Hegelian idealism, the view that ideas move history.[4] The second is Lockean individualism, the view that the autonomous and rational individual is the key factor in social change.[5] The third is Christian pietism, the view that the most important goal in life is having a heart that is right before God. While Hunter believes these to be important, he also believes that strategies based upon them will fail. He believes that conversion is essential but not enough to base a movement on—one that would change societies and the direction of an entire nation.

Hunter posits the following principles for how to bring about cultural change:

1. The key actor in history is not individual genius but the network and the new institutions that are created out of those networks. He points to the outlawing of slavery in England. Most would contend that its victory was due to the character of William Wilberforce. Hunter, however, says it was the Clapham Circle, a powerful network of Christian abolitionists, that carried the day. He says that charismatic figures play a role but that it is the network that gets it done.

2. The individuals, networks, and institutions most critically involved in the production of culture operate at the center, where prestige is the highest, not on the periphery, where status is low. In other words, if the president of Harvard believes the right thing, he will have more impact and cause more change than a plumber who holds the same view.

3. Long-term cultural change always occurs from the top down. It is the work of elites, of the gatekeepers who provide creative direction and management to the leading institutions of society. This would challenge the idea that grassroots movements bring about great change. Hunter suggests that the Renaissance, the Reformation, The Great Awakenings, the Enlightenment, the triumph of capitalism over mercantilism and feudalism, and all of the democratic revolutions in the West began among elites and then percolated into the larger society. (One wonders where the anti-war movement came from during Vietnam. Were the students in the streets the key, or was it politicians and professors? Was the early church movement successful because of elite contacts and infiltration or because of the character of the people?) I also wonder why Jesus gave instructions to make disciples of all nations and that the end would not come until the gospel of the kingdom was preached to the entire world (see Matthew 24:14). It seems that Jesus believed dramatic change could be achieved through evangelism.

4. World change is most intense when the networks of elites and the institutions they lead overlap. Again and again we see that the impetus, energy, and direction for changing the world is found where cultural, economic, and often political resources overlap, where networks of elites who generate these various resources come together in common purpose.[6]

Who Do We Believe and What Difference Does It Make?

As was pointed out earlier, the early church did change the world. I can't imagine its members sitting around plotting a strategy that focused on networks, elites, and gatekeepers. Those in power were trying to kill them, throw them in jail, and put an end to their efforts. It seems obvious that Jesus chose marginalized, observant Jews who came from the working class; he did not choose the elite of society. These early Christians stumbled their way through his teaching; they were slow to learn, slower still to unlearn. But even so, they changed the world. The change was not on Main Street. It was largely under the radar for the first three hundred years. It wasn't until Christianity was proclaimed the official religion of Rome that the victory had been won.

Some would argue that even though Christianity became the official religion, it didn't change the world—at least in the way more contemporary efforts to engage culture talk about. Earlier I mentioned an author who asks some penetrating questions about the global problems of hunger, poverty, AIDS, regional wars, tribal rivalries, and runaway greed and how we might address them. In my view, this author expands the Great Commission to include cultural change much like Hunter describes cultural change.

There is a school of thought among serious Christian thinkers that is attempting to bring together the Christian left and right to mount a more holistic and powerful mission to the world. Its strength is calling both sides to engage the problems together. The left has a history of going directly to the needy and meeting temporal needs without preconditions. The right has built the hospitals, fed the hungry, and done many of the same things as the left but has used it for an opportunity to proclaim the gospel. Here is the danger in this. At some point, in order to address all the issues, these two sides will disagree about the content of the gospel and whether it should be preached at all.

I am not one who believes that every act of kindness needs a parallel presentation of the gospel. I think such a precondition of compassion does not square with Jesus himself and his life. I tremble as I ask these questions: *Are we expecting too much? Are we expecting a different outcome in our culture than the Bible promises? Are we being wooed into the post-millennial idea of ushering in the kingdom of God through becoming a better people and society?* The book of Revelation speaks of a thousand-year reign of Christ. Of the faithful it says, "They all came to life again, and they reigned with Christ for a thousand years" (20:4). This will be a period when people live in the best of conditions, in as perfect an environment as is possible. But when the thousand-year duration ends, Satan is let out of his prison. He will deceive the nations and lead one final rebellion against God. This seems to end any hope of utopia, a word coined by Thomas More in 1516 that means "no place." The nature of human personality does not permit such a belief. Complete transformation comes only by passing through the veil of death. As long as humans, religious or not, are what humans are, with an embedded sin nature, there can be no earthly utopia. Evil must be eliminated, and that includes the evil in human hearts, which will require more than transformation of human personality. It will require a personality fit for eternity, one absent of sin.

I can hear the protests now: "So you are advocating capitulation, that we don't try to change the world around us." No. I think we should seek to be the salt and light to the world. We should dedicate ourselves to helping every strata of society, especially the suffering and the poor. As I said already, there doesn't need to be a corresponding gospel presentation for every act of kindness, but we should keep in mind that mission one is the Great Commission. The mark of the Christian society is love; it is disciples giving themselves to others, regardless of the cost. We are constrained to do all this within the clear instructions of Jesus to make disciples, "baptizing them in the name of the Father and of the Son and of the Holy Spirit, and teaching them to obey everything [he has] commanded [us]" (Matthew 28:19-20, NIV).

The focus is making followers of Jesus who are changed by the new life in Christ in them. Without this internal change, all other change is temporal and inferior. There must be a priority of mission; otherwise, we will find ourselves living with a delusion that better living conditions can bring us the utopian idea that is millennial life.

Christianity became the dominant religion in the Greco-Roman world by 350, but it didn't prevent the Roman world from collapse. In 410, when Augustine was fifty-six years old, he heard the news that Rome had been sacked and he wrote, "Don't lose heart, brothers. There will be an end to every earthly kingdom, and if this is actually the end now, God sees."[7] For the rest of his life, Augustine worked on his masterpiece *The City of God*, describing what we could actually expect redemption to do for the world: "The life in this City is utterly and entirely a life of fellowship."[8]

But alas, such words didn't stop the church from becoming corrupt. It seems that no matter how much the church has thrived, it has been a mixed blessing. As Elton Trueblood wrote more than forty years ago, "The hardest problem of Christianity is the problem of the church. We cannot live without it, and we cannot live with it. In practice the local congregation is nearly always disappointing."[9]

I contend that the key to changing the world is a vibrant transformation on the inside that focuses on a person at one with Christ. I would argue that the elite will be infiltrated informally through relationships and divine appointments, which is what happened in the early church. Here's how it works: A follower of Jesus is seated next to the chairman of the Joint Chiefs of Staff on a flight and introduces the general to Christ, or a limo driver influences an international film star to follow Christ. This is the way we will change the world, one person at a time. It is more organic than organizational; it is the common person, such as a young Rick Warren, who then builds a worldwide network. I believe that Hunter is describing the result of such infiltration. Dallas Willard would agree. He writes, "Widespread transformation of character through wisely disciplined discipleship to Christ can transform our world. It can disarm the structural evils that have always dominated humankind and now threaten to destroy the world."[10]

So I would say to all who care, let's address the social ills of our day, but let's also never forget our motive. It is Christ taking hold inside. Jesus is the inside man; he lives in us because that is where transformation begins. But that is not where it ends.

As we've seen throughout this book, change always shows up in the way we relate to others. Transformation isn't a short-term experience; it lasts all of our lives. Its basis is the development of a spiritual heart that fosters a life of uncomplicated obedience. It is not a passive life but one of sustained effort. It will require tools, structure, and discipline. It is also a life of suffering for many because they follow Christ, for all of us because we are human. Most of all, it means living in community with others, because in order for transformation into the image of Christ to have meaning, we must seek to serve and love others. In order to make a difference, we need to be different.

Notes

Introduction

1. Dallas Willard, *The Divine Conspiracy: Rediscovering Our Hidden Life in God* (New York: HarperCollins, 1998).
2. C. S. Lewis, *Mere Christianity* (New York: Macmillian, 1952), 191.

Chapter 1: Rethinking What It Means to Be Christian

1. See Galatians 1:6-9,11. "I did not receive it from man, nor was I taught it, but it came through a revelation of Jesus Christ" (1:12, RSV).
2. Paul Weton, comp., *Lesslie Newbigin: Missionary Theologian: A Reader* (Grand Rapids, MI: Eerdmans, 2006), 52.
3. Acts 22–28. Paul makes four presentations.
4. Tim Keller, "The Gospel in All Its Forms," *Leadership Journal*, Spring 2008, 78.
5. Dietrich Bonhoeffer, *The Cost of Discipleship* (New York: Macmillian, 1949), 57.
6. My current view is a somewhat nuanced version of that view. I thought in broader categories than I do now (for example, on the issue of authority of women in the church). Then I might have said that women should not have authority in the church. Today I would suggest that means ultimate authority. That still would not

make both poles of this issue happy, but that is where I am.

7. Brian McLaren, *Everything Must Change* (Nashville: Thomas Nelson, 2007), 144.

8. Phyllis Tickle, *The Great Emergence: How Christianity Is Changing and Why* (San Francisco: Jossey-Bass, 2008), 69.

9. Tickle, 1-1.

10. Tickle, 162.

11. David T. Olson, *The American Church in Crisis: Groundbreaking Research Based on a National Database of over 200,000 Churches* (Grand Rapids, MI: Zondervan, 2005), 36.

12. Bill Hull, *Straight Talk on Spiritual Power: Experiencing the Fullness of God in the Church* (Grand Rapids, MI: Baker, 2002).

13. Tyler Wigg-Stevenson, "Jesus Is Not a Brand," *Christianity Today*, January 2009, vol. 53, num. 1, 20.

14. Dallas Willard, *The Spirit of the Disciplines: Understanding How God Changes Lives* (San Francisco: Harper and Row, 1989), 221.

15. Rodney Stark, *The Rise of Christianity: How the Obscure, Marginal Jesus Movement Became the Dominant Religious Force* (San Francisco: HarperOne, 1997), 3.

Chapter 2: The Gospel of the Kingdom

1. Matthew 3:2—the kingdom of God is near; Matthew 6:10—pray for the kingdom to come; Matthew 7:21—people were invited to enter into the kingdom; Matthew 6:33—seek it first; John 18:36—the kingdom is not of this world. Jesus' disciples asked him when he would restore the kingdom (see Acts 1:6), and Paul taught about the kingdom in Rome (see Acts 28:31).

2. Dallas Willard, *Renovation of the Heart: Putting On the Character of Christ* (Colorado Springs: NavPress, 2002), 38.

3. Keller Tim, "The Gospel in All Its Forms," *Leadership Journal*, Spring 2008, 76.

4. Philip Jenkins, *The Next Christendom: The Coming of Global*

Christianity (New York: Oxford University Press, 2002), 211.

5. Bruce Metzger, *The New Testament: Its Background, Growth, and Content* (Nashville: Abingdon, 1965), 172. Metzger points out six summary statements in Acts: 6:7; 9:31; 12:24; 16:5; 19:20, and 28:31. A summary of the summaries would be that the church multiplied, or grew and multiplied, or strengthened and increased in numbers daily, or the Word of God prevailed and grew, that the teaching of the kingdom of God and Jesus Christ was done openly and unhindered. To get hard numbers, one must go to historical studies and records outside the Scriptures.

6. Rodney Stark, *The Rise of Christianity: How the Obscure, Marginal Jesus Movement Became the Dominant Religious Force* (San Francisco: HarperOne, 1997), 7.

7. Stark, 154.

8. Stark, 174.

9. Stark, 181.

10. Stark, 177.

11. Dallas Willard, *The Spirit of the Disciplines: Understanding How God Changes Lives* (San Francisco: Harper and Row, 1988), xi.

12. Philip Jenkins, *The Next Christendom*: *The Coming Of Global Christianity* (New York: Oxford University Press, 2002), 220.

Chapter 3: A Messy, Lifelong Journey

1. Chris Hedges, *I Don't Believe in Atheists* (New York: Free Press, 2008), 114.

2. Flesh as body (see Galatians 2:20), as futile human effort (see Galatians 3:3), as the enemy of God (see Galatians 5:16-17).

3. George Fox, *Journal of George Fox*, ed. Norman Penney (London: Dent, 1948), 91.

4. http://www.cas.sc.edu/hist/faculty/edwardsk/hist310/reader /providence.pdf

5. Paul was fond of the metaphor that an athlete must go into "strict training." This is where he is clear about the relationship of

training to causing one's body and its natural desires to serve the purposes of God in one's life. Elton Trueblood often said that discipline was the key to freedom from slavery to self.

6. Galatians 2:20 describes the mystery of Christ living through a person. It is the person but somehow only with our cooperation in faith and intention. The wrestling comes from Ephesians 6:10-18, and the idea of the flesh or the Enemy scoring is evident from 1 John 1:9–2:2.

7. Peter Martin, *Samuel Johnson: A Biography* (Cambridge: The Belknap Press of Harvard University Press, 2008), 343.

Chapter 4: A Disciple's Focus

1. Dietrich Bonhoeffer, *The Cost of Discipleship* (New York: Macmillan, 1963), 63.

2. See 2 Corinthians 5:17; Colossians 1:27; 2:9; John 14:18.

3. The first ecumenical synod was Nicea (325 AD). It condemned Arianism, a heresy that denied the divinity of Christ. The second synod of Constantinople (381 AD) condemned the idea that the Holy Spirit was not divine. The third synod at Ephesus (431 AD) condemned Nestorianism, a heresy that separated the divine and human natures of Christ. The fourth synod (451 AD) condemned the teaching that Christ possessed only a divine nature.

4. C. S. Lewis, *Mere Christianity* (New York: Macmillian, 1952), 30.

5. Discipline yourself for godliness (see 1 Timothy 4:7). The example of godliness is Jesus. Paul exhorted his followers to imitate him and to follow him as he followed Christ (see 1 Corinthians 4:14-16; 11:1). Paul also explained that the goal of his work was Christian maturity, Christ being formed in every follower (see Colossians 1:28; Galatians 4:19). He described the growing process as a progression from one degree to the next degree all sponsored by the Holy Spirit (see 2 Corinthians 3:18). Peter took up this same idea in 1 Peter 1:3-7; 2:21-24; 2 Peter 1:3-9. This entire journey makes possible a state called "spiritual

maturity," which is another way of saying that you are being shaped into a little Christ. The writer of Hebrews provided the process of practice, practice, practice as a way to gain spiritual maturity.

6. Rodney Stark, *The Rise of Christianity: How the Obscure, Marginal Jesus Movement Became the Dominant Religious Force* (San Francisco: HarperOne, 1997), 176.

7. John Coe, "Spiritual Formation Lecture Series," March 2006, Talbot School of Theology, notes page 5.

8. Coe, 6.

9. No condemnation for those in Christ (see Romans 8:1). This is preceded by Paul's lamentation about the give and take of sin and the weakness of the human condition. He thanked God that he alone can rescue him from the "body of death." The entire argument of Romans 6–8 is saying that God stands with us in our battle with sin and that our improved performance will come as a result of our life in the Spirit. First Corinthians 15:58 gives the exhortation to be "steadfast, immovable, always abounding in the work of the Lord, knowing that in the Lord your labor is not in vain" (RSV).

10. "'God opposes the proud but favors the humble.' So humble yourselves before God. Resist the devil, and he will flee from you. Come close to God, and God will come close to you" (James 4:6-8). First Peter 5:5-7 is very much the same exhortation. Humility attracts God's grace.

11. Bonhoeffer, 69

12. John R. W. Stott, *The Cross of Christ* (Chicago: Downers Grove, IL: InterVarsity, 1986), 160.

Chapter 5: Real Change Always "Shows Up"

1. Dallas Willard, "Spiritual Formation: What It Is, and How It Is Done," www.dwillard.org (emphasis added).

2. C. S. Lewis, *The Screwtape Letters: And Screwtape Proposes a Toast*

(New York: Macmillan, 1962), 11.

3. Willard (emphasis added).
4. Rueben P. Job and Norman Shawchuck, *A Guide to Prayer for Ministers and Other Servants* (Nashville: The Upper Room, 1983), 133.
5. Karl Barth, *The Word of God and the Word of Man* (Sidney A. Weston, 1928), 9.

Chapter 6: The Only Path to Spiritual Transformation

1. Peter Martin, *Samuel Johnson: A Biography* (Cambridge: The Belknap Press of Harvard University Press, 2008), 457–458.
2. Dallas Willard, notes from Plenary Address at the Spiritual Formation Forum, Los Angeles, May 13, 2004.
3. It's generally understood that the canon of the New Testament was settled through a letter written by Bishop Athanasius to other Bishops. He was held in such high respect that his studied opinion was the final word during that period. 397 AD.
4. "Complete" in 2 Timothy 3:17 (RSV) is *artios,* meaning "to be fit for all good works." That fitness is more than skill. It also is used in a compound form translated as equipped later in the verse, which indicates an emphasis on skill, fully outfitted, supplied.
5. Galatians 4:19; Romans 12:2; and Romans 8:29 (RSV) speak of formed, transformed, and conformed respectively with the basic Greek word *morphe.* This is the origin of the English word *form.*

Chapter 7: Being with God

1. Among some Christians, there is an unhealthy attraction to romanticize our relationship to Christ. The spiritual formation movement, with its mystical quality, extols Saint Catherine of Siena and others who suffered delusions and even mystical sexual experiences with Christ that would make the most urbane woman blush. I think God is competent to address himself to a wide variety of people who are attracted to various

parts of his personality. The danger is taking any of it too far to accommodate our personalities.

Chapter 8: Reading His Word

1. This book is destined to be a classic. I would recommend you read it now; it is a wonderful read and will make you ravenous for God's Word.
2. Eugene Peterson, *Eat This Book: A Conversation in the Art of Spiritual Reading* (Grand Rapids, MI: Eerdmans, 2006), xi.
3. Peterson, xi.
4. Romans 12:2 and 1 Corinthians 2:1-16 speak of the transformed mind and acquiring the mind of Christ. Hebrews 5:11-14 speaks of milk and meat, that God's Word is essential to that process which is spiritual exercise and the acquisition of spiritual discernment. First Peter 2:2 teaches the need for nourishment, and 2 Timothy 3:16 claims that the Word of God is central to all spiritual development.
5. Greg Hawkins and Cally Parkinson, *Reveal Follow Me* (Barrington, IL: Willow Creek Publishing, 2008), 41.
6. Peterson, 14.
7. Peterson, 104.
8. Bruce Demarest, *Satisfy Your Soul: Renewing the Heart of Christian Spirituality* (Colorado Springs, CO: NavPress, 2000), 136–137.
9. Peterson, 28–30.
10. Peterson, 11.

Chapter 9: Hearing His Voice

1. Dallas Willard, *In Search of Guidance: Developing a Conversational Relationship with God* (Grand Rapids, MI: Zondervan, 1993), 179.
2. Frederick Meyer spent the last few years of his life working as a pastor in England's churches but still made trips to North

America, including one he made at age eighty (his earlier evangelistic tours had included South Africa and Asia as well as the United States and Canada). A few days before his death, Meyer wrote the following words to a friend:

> I have just heard, to my great surprise, that I have but a few days to live. It may be that before this reaches you, I shall have entered the palace. Don't trouble to write. We shall meet in the morning. (from Wikipedia.org)

Following F. B. Meyer's death in 1929, an English newspaper, *The Daily Telegraph*, described him as "The Archbishop of the Free Churches." He had earlier been described in the *New York Observer* as "a man of international fame whose services are constantly sought by churches over the wide and increasing empire of Christendom." In 2007, Stephen Timms wrote of him as a man with *enduring popularity*, dubbed *virtually a Christian socialist.* (from Wikipedia.org)

3. F. B. Meyer, *The Secret of Guidance* (Chicago: Moody, 2007), 14–15.
4. Willard, 187.
5. E. Stanley Jones, *A Song of Ascents*, 190, quoted in Willard, 188.
6. See John 2; 5:31-47; 8:54-59; Matthew 23
7. Willard, 191.
8. Willard, 192.
9. Isn't it interesting that Satan accuses us before the throne of God day and night? He is preoccupied with stealing what is good in this life from us. God asks us to move forward. Lucifer's focus is the past, the guilt, the failure and shame that are part of the human condition.
10. Alan Jacobs, *The Narnian: The Life and Imagination of C. S. Lewis* (San Francisco: HarperOne, 2005), 133.

Chapter 10: The Development of the Spiritual Heart

1. James R. Newby, *Elton Trueblood: Believer, Teacher, and Friend* (San Francisco: Harper and Row, 1990), 55.

2. C. S. Lewis, *The Weight of Glory* (San Francisco: Harper and Row, 2001), 26, quoted in Rueben P. Job and Norman Shawchuck, *A Guide to Prayer for Ministers and Other Servants* (Nashville: The Upper Room, 1983), 85.
3. Franz Delitzsch, *A System of Biblical Psychology* (Grand Rapids, MI: Baker, 1977), 292.
4. Delitzsch, 292.
5. Delitzsch, 293–294.
6. Richard Foster, "Spiritual Formation Agenda," *Christianity Today*, January 2009, vol. 53, 30.
7. William Law, *A Serious Call to a Devout and Holy Life*, 44.
8. Law, 27.
9. Law, 16.
10. Foster, 30.

Chapter 11: Uncomplicated Obedience
1. Richard Foster, "Spiritual Formation Agenda," *Christianity Today*, January 2009, vol. 53, 30.
2. Dallas Willard, *The Spirit of the Disciplines: Understanding How God Changes Lives* (San Francisco: Harper and Row, 1989), xi.
3. Examples: Galatians, the entire book, but especially 4:17–5:25, and 1 Corinthians 3:1-3. The very comparison and contrast in Romans 6–8 is indicative of the continuing struggle. There could be a distinction drawn, however, between Paul's personal life and the struggles of others. But the book of 2 Corinthians indicates a great deal of personal struggle for the apostle, a struggle having to do with personal peace. It was easy for Paul to obey Christ, but his life was not easy.
4. Dallas Willard, quoted in Bill Hull, *Choose the Life: Exploring a Faith That Embraces Discipleship* (Grand Rapids, MI: Baker, 2004), 6.
5. See John 5:19-23; 17:1-5; Luke 23:34,46; Matthew 26:38-44.
6. Malcolm Muggeridge, *A Third Testament* (New York: Little, Brown, 1976), 58.

Chapter 12: Sustained Effort

1. See 1 Corinthians 9:24-27; Colossians 1:28-29; 1 Timothy 4:7; Hebrews 5:14; Galatians 6:7-9.
2. There is a good deal of variety for who includes what disciplines and how they are categorized. Please see *The Celebration of the Disciplines* by Richard Foster or *The Spirit of the Disciplines* by Dallas Willard for additional information.
3. The monastic period is generally believed to have begun in the fifth century with the bishop of Rome, later to be known as Gregory the Great, who encouraged the literacy and disciplines necessary to sustain the Christian faith.
4. Prayed alone (see Mark 1:35); fasted alone, the temptation in the wilderness (see Matthew 4:1-11); lived a life of frugality (see Luke 9:57-62); sacrifice, humility, submission (see Philippians 2:5-8); memorized Scripture and his understanding of it as a boy and then as a teacher (see Luke 2:41-48; Matthew 5:17-48); chastity was the record of his life and he practiced secrecy. He kept his own counsel regarding his purpose and life until the proper time as recorded in Mark 8:31. Yes, the monastics made a list and became legalistic about these practices, but to believe in their power to change us one only needs the example of Jesus.
5. Dallas Willard, *The Spirit of the Disciplines: Understanding How God Changes Lives* (San Francisco: Harper and Row, 1989), 10.
6. This idea is unique to Christian spiritual formation.
7. Dietrich Bonhoeffer, *The Cost of Discipleship* (New York: Macmillian, 1949), 69.

Chapter 13: Structure and Accountability in Community

1. Dietrich Bonhoeffer, *Life Together: The Classic Exploration of Faith in Community* (San Francisco: Harper and Row, 1954), 23. Originally published in Germany in 1938. This was the work of Bonhoeffer based on life together at the Confessing Church Seminary. The seminary was established for two years before it

was closed by the Gestapo. Bonhoeffer's genius for deep insight and the turning of a phrase is in full bloom as he describes the seminarians' community for the twenty-five vicars.

2. Proposition 8 was on the ballot in California in 2008. Its purpose was to define marriage as the union of one man and one woman. The gay community and many others considered it a civil rights issue and voted against the measure. There has subsequently been a great deal of pushback because the proposition passed. The Internet play is part of that countersurge.

3. Dietrich Bonhoeffer, *A Testament to Freedom: The Essential Writings of Dietrich Bonhoeffer* (San Francisco: HarperOne, 1995), 407.

4. Bonhoeffer, *Life Together*, 78.

5. Greg Hawkins and Cally Parkinson, *Reveal* study and *Follow Me* (Barrington, IL: Willow Creek Association, 2008), 90, 88.

6. Hawkins and Parkinson, 36.

7. Rodney Stark, *Cities of God: The Real Story of How Christianity Became an Urban Movement and Conquered Rome* (San Francisco: Harper One, 2007), 13.

8. Lesslie Newbigin, *The Gospel in a Pluralist Society* (Grand Rapids, MI: Eerdmans, 1990).

9. Bill Thrall and Bruce McNicol, "Forming the High Trust Culture" (Leadership Catalyst Publishing, 2000), Section on Submission, A-10.

Chapter 14: Can a Privatized Spirituality Change the World?

1. Elton Trueblood's work *The Incendiary Fellowship* is a wonderful book that speaks of the fire of the true spiritual life and how it affects the faith community and the public square.

2. Elton Trueblood, *The Incendiary Fellowshop* (San Francisco: Harper and Row, 1967), 108.

3. Malcolm Muggeridge, *A Third Testament* (New York: Orbis Books, 1976), 32.

4. Freidrich Hegel, a German teacher and writer, best known for his work *Phenomenology of Spirit*. He held the prestigious chair of philosophy at Berlin University for ten years.

5. John Locke (August 29, 1632–October 28, 1704) was an English philosopher. Locke is considered the first of the British empiricists but is equally important to social contract theory. His ideas had enormous influence on the development of epistemology and political philosophy, and he is widely regarded as one of the most influential Enlightenment thinkers.

6. James Davidson Hunter, as reported in Address to Trinity Forum, June 21–22, 2002. Summarized by Jay Lorensen on June 10, 2006, in Leadership Movements, Marks of a Movement, www .onmovements.com.

7. Muggeridge, 17.

8. Muggeridge, 22.

9. Trueblood, 77.

10. Dallas Willard, *The Spirit of the Disciplines: Understanding How God Changes Lives* (San Francisco: Harper and Row, 1989), xi.

Author

BILL HULL'S efforts as a pastor and writer have been focused on being a disciple and making disciples. He has written several groundbreaking books for leaders and churches. Bill and his wife Jane have been married since 1969 and are the parents of two grown sons. To learn more about Bill and his work go to www.BillHull.com.

ALSO BY
BILL HULL

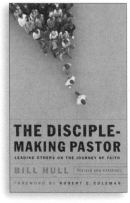

The Disciple-Making Pastor,
rev. & exp. ed.

BakerBooks

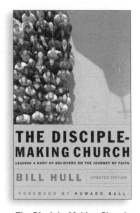

The Disciple-Making Church,
updated ed.

BakerBooks

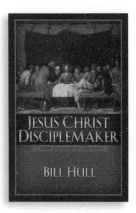

Jesus Christ, Disciplemaker,
20th ann. ed.

BakerBooks

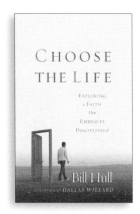

Choose the Life

BakerBooks

Building High Commitment
in a Low-Commitment World

ℛ Revell

BAKER PUBLISHING GROUP

www.bakerpublishinggroup.com

Read more on discipleship, culture, and theory.

The Complete Book of Discipleship
Bill Hull

978-1-57683-897-6

The Complete Book of Discipleship is the definitive A-to-Z resource on discipleship for every Christian. This well-organized, indexed guide pulls together such topics as spiritual growth, transformation, spiritual disciplines, and discipleship in the local church and beyond.

The Kingdom Life
978-1-60006-280-3

Bill Hull comes together with a dozen other spiritual formation leaders—Dallas Willard, Bruce Demarest, Bill Thrall, and others—to create a collection of wisdom and honest personal revelation in the areas of discipleship and spiritual formation. The uniqueness of the book is its three-pronged focus on transformation, community, and outreach.

Dictionary of Everyday Theology and Culture
Bruce Demarest and Keith J. Matthews, general editors

978-1-60006-192-9

This resource provides everyday people a guide to understanding Christian theology and key social and cultural issues in the contemporary world. With a practical focus, it helps readers understand core Christian truths that provide the framework of the Christian worldview and apply these truths to life and service as followers of Jesus.

To order copies, call NavPress at 1-800-366-7788 or
log on to www.navpress.com.